The HEALING POWER *of* PRAYER

BRIDGET MARY MEEHAN

LIGUORI
PUBLICATIONS

ONE LIGUORI DRIVE
LIGUORI, MO 63057-9999
(314) 464-2500

Liguori Publications
Liguori, Missouri

Library of Congress Cataloging-in-Publication Data
Meehan, Bridget Mary.
     The healing power of prayer / Bridget Mary Meehan.
         p. cm.
     Originally published in 1988.
     ISBN 0-89243-866-5 (pbk.)
       1. Spiritual Healing. 2. Prayer—Christianity. I. Title.
[BT732.5.M44 1995]
242'.8—dc20   95-45412

Dedication to my family:

my parents, Bridie and Jack, my Aunt Molly McCarthy, my brothers Sean and Patrick, my sisters-in-law Nancy and Valerie, my niece and nephew Katie and Danny.

To my friends and mentors:

especially Regina Madonna Oliver, Irene Marshall, Sandra Voelker, Marcia Tibbitts, Betty Wade, Susan Curcio, Patricia Byrne, Patricia McAleavy, Kathleen Bulger, Maria Bonard, Eileen Dohn, Josephine Pida, Phyllis and Wendell Hurst, Peg and Bob Bowen, Estelle Spachman, Jutta Clark, Alicia Clark, Christina Clark, Rosemary Walsh, Elizabeth Hoisington, Debbie Dubuque, Joe Mulqueen, John Weyand, Francis Keete, Mary and Kevin Fitzgibbons, Megan Fitzgibbons, Patricia Herlihy, Mary Guertin, Dick Guertin, Mary Kay and John Salomone, Kathleen Wiesberg, Donna Mogan, Nancy Healy, Maureen Milnamow, Olga Gane, Evelyn Mulhall, Mary Patricia Mulhall, Kathleen Mulhall, Eileen Kelly, Eugenia Garrido, Virginia Limon, Dawn Vehmeier, Anna Minassian, Ellen Coakley, Cornelius Coakley, Helen Groff, Luz and Rafael Sandiego, Dorothy Vail, Roseanne Fedorko, Lynn Johnson, Daisy Sullivan, Michal Morches, Jeanette Kraska, Maria and Steve Billick, Doris Mason, Jojo and Douglas Sandiego, Consilia Karli, Kaye Brown, Carol and Ray Buchanan, Leo Shulten, Fritz and Barbara Warren, Mike Marshall, Larry Skummer, the Sisters For Christian Community

To all Celtic women and men in my family:

Noreen and Ger Davy, Molly Meehan, Peg Meehan, Mary D. and John Meehan, Mary and Bernie Ferns, Rev. Seamus Meehan, Pat and Eileen Meehan, Margaret and Aidan Ryan, Mary and Allan Tregent, Rose and Tim Meehan, Elizabeth and Martin Brophy, Kathleen and Christy Donnelly, Esther Meehan, Tess Murphy, Rev. Adrian McNamara, Kathleen and Desmond McNamara, Roy Meehan, John Meehan, Mary Meehan, Alice and Sean Meehan, and Eileen Preston.

To Kass Dotterweich, editor at Liguori, with gratitude.

CONTENTS

AN OPEN LETTER *to* THOSE *in* NEED *of* HEALING

Healing is big news! Whether it's the gospel story of Jesus healing a crippled person or the modern-day healing of a troubled heart, healing can be a faith-filled event that changes lives and works wonders.

Recent years have seen a tremendous increase in an awareness of the value and importance of inner healing prayer. The charismatic renewal, Cursillo groups, prayer communities, and other renewal movements have all played a part in this phenomenon. The realization that, more and more people hurt mentally, emotionally, physically, and spiritually has heightened the need for healing, forgiveness, and peace. Sickness and disease, violence and warfare, tension and stress, alcohol abuse and drugs, jobs and finances, families and friends: all cause pain and suffering that cry out for healing. In response to this need many Christian churches have developed programs and ministries designed to help people find God's healing. These efforts have revived traditional truths about healing and generated new ways to bring the power of healing into the lives of today's Christians.

Just as there are all types of people and a multitude of pains that need healing, there are many ways to pray and find healing through prayer. Each individual is unique and has his or her own way of praying. As you become familiar with the innovative and exciting approaches to inner healing prayer as explained here, you can eventually select the method that seems best suited to you. The key to discovering healing through prayer is to be flexible and avoid "canonizing" one particular method. If a certain style fits your spiritual needs for experiencing God's healing more deeply than another, rely on it; if it doesn't fit or feel comfortable, choose another approach.

This book offers you the opportunity to experience divine healing in a variety of settings. You may want to read the prayer experiences on your own and use the reflection questions for private meditation. You might also consider discussing your ideas in small groups, with your spouse, or with a good friend. Regardless of the method you select, this book is intended to help you develop:

- a greater awareness of the variety of prayer approaches that can be used in inner healing prayer

- a clearer understanding of the value of imagination and prayer in the process of inner healing

- a deeper appreciation of inner healing prayer as a powerful tool in dealing with the problems of anxiety, anger, rejection, stress, and loneliness

- a greater realization of the effectiveness and richness of inner healing prayer as a means of spiritual growth

- an increased ability to rely on various approaches to prayer as effective means of inner healing in daily life

If we are to appreciate the many different approaches to healing prayer, however, we must understand the historical and biblical framework of healing in the Church. Part One offers a historical overview and explains Jesus' outlook on healing, the Church's teachings about healing, the relationship between healing and salvation, and the role of redemptive suffering in the life of Christians. It also presents a practical rationale for inner healing prayer and suggests ways to find healing in everyday life.

Part Two presents ten different healing prayer experiences:

1. Healing-of-Memories Prayer: inviting Jesus into a painful memory with his healing grace

2. Forgiveness Prayer: asking Jesus for reconciliation and healing through the power of his Cross

3. Journal Prayer: using the intuitive powers of the mind to reveal the presence of God within human experience

4. Centering Prayer: passing beyond thoughts, images, and feelings to unite your heart and will with God

5. Scripture Prayer: moving into the details and emotions of a biblical passage to listen to God speaking personally from within the text

6. Fantasy Prayer (guided imagery prayer): using the imagination to set the stage for a prayerful encounter with God

7. Relaxation Prayer: releasing stress to God and discovering God's abiding and loving presence

8. Healing Affirmations for Daily Living: touching the divine wisdom within

9. Prayer for Healing Families, Races, Nations, Religions and Earth: expanding consciousness to fully know that God is Love and that when you love you are a birther of new energy that makes miracles happen

10. Prayer of the Sufferer: encountering God's saving power in the midst of pain, unanswered questions, and puzzling mysteries

This book does not advocate a theoretical approach that merely teaches *about* inner healing prayer. Rather, it attempts to integrate a practical theological perspective with a creative experiential approach. This book is written with the conviction that we learn to pray by praying, not by reading or talking about prayer.

It is also written from the conviction that healing prayer is an attainable life-changing force. As we realize the healing love of God in our lives, we can begin to view life from the perspective of Jesus Christ. We can experience a new freedom that destroys the bonds that shackle us, learn to forgive and ask forgiveness with greater courage, become more aware of our own brokenness and limitations, and develop greater sensitivity to the needs of others.

I hope you will reap rich rewards from this exploration into inner healing prayer and from the experience of embracing God, Healer of our lives and of our world.

BRIDGET MARY MEEHAN, SSFC

PART ONE

HEALING IN THE JUDEO-CHRISTIAN TRADITION

Chapter 1

A BIBLICAL VIEW of HEALING

Some of the most popular stories in the Hebrew Scriptures (Old Testament) demonstrate the Lord Yahweh's healing power. The early books of the Bible tell how the power of God brought healing and wholeness to barren, hurting women through the gift of children (to Sarah, Genesis 18:10,14; to Manoah's wife, the mother of Samson, Judges 13:5, 24; to Hannah, the mother of Samuel, 1 Samuel 1:19-20; and to the Shunammite woman, 2 Kings 4:16-17).

Both Elijah and Elisha, two of Israel's more famous prophets, healed an innocent child (1 Kings 17:17-23; 2 Kings 4:18-37) through actions that closely resembled the healing activities of Jesus recorded in the New Testament. Elisha's cleansing of Naaman the leper was another incident where a special healing was granted to a good person who had done nothing to deserve the sickness and pain he suffered (2 Kings 5:1-15).

Many of the psalms call us to have trust in the Holy One as a healer of mind, body, and spirit (Psalms 41,46,62,74,116,121, and 147). While these psalms proclaim divine healing power, Psalms 73 and 94 protest the fact that God has not rewarded goodness with healing or happiness.

Isaiah often encouraged his listeners to hope for the day of Yahweh when all illnesses would be healed. The blind and deaf would see and hear, and the dead would come back to life (Isaiah 26:19; 29:18; 61:1-11).

Then will the eyes of the blind be opened,
the ears of the deaf be cleared;
Then will the lame leap like a stag,
then the tongue of the dumb will sing.

ISAIAH 35:5-6

While some people viewed this day of Yahweh as the end of time when all wrongs would be corrected, others associated it with the coming of the Messiah who would initiate the Reign of the new age marked by peace and fulfillment.

Physical healings and inner healing prayer are rooted in the Hebrew Scripture's anticipation of the Messiah and in Jesus' approach to his ministry. In his willingness to bring healing and peace, Jesus echoed the thoughts of Isaiah about the importance of healing. Jesus embraced and accepted human sufferings, sorrows, and faults. He understood the shortcomings and sins that plagued human beings, and saw how they caused physical, spiritual, mental, and emotional pain. Jesus also saw how a great deal of human suffering was not related to any type of sin or moral failing, but to natural disasters and physical ailments. In his infinite wisdom, the Messiah went beyond the "spiritual" side of sin and ministered to the total person who was wounded and in need of healing. This fulfilled the prophecy about the Messiah that Isaiah recorded in his fourth Song of the Suffering Servant:

> *Yet it was our infirmities that he bore,*
> *our sufferings that he endured,*
> *While we thought of him as stricken,*
> *as one smitten by God and afflicted.*
> *But he was pierced for our offenses,*
> *crushed for our sins,*
> *Upon him was the chastisement that makes us*
> *whole,*
> *by his stripes we were healed.*

ISAIAH 53:4-5

Chapter 2

JESUS' OUTLOOK *on* HEALING

Jesus saw healing as a manifestation of God's compassion toward sick and sinful people. Through his healing ministry, Jesus revealed God's divine, saving love present in the world. This attitude of concern, which first appeared in the Hebrew Scriptures, was powerfully revealed through Jesus and has continually been manifested throughout the history of the Church.

Jesus viewed healing as an inseparable part of the proclamation of the Good News. The gospels of Mark, Matthew, and Luke divide the ministry of Jesus into three categories: preaching, teaching, and healing. As Jesus healed people who were sick in mind and body, he gave a clear sign by word and action of the power of God that had broken through into the world. In fact, Jesus frequently emphasized that his healing ministry was a sign that the Reign of God was breaking forth.

Jesus made it clear, however, that he operated through the power of

God. In answer to the charge that he was a sorcerer, Jesus replied:

> *And if I drive out demons by Beelzebul, by whom do*
> *your own people drive them out? Therefore they will be*
> *your judges. But if it is by the Spirit of God that I drive*
> *out demons, then the [Reign] of God has come upon*
> *you.*

> MATTHEW 12:27-28

Healing: An Important Task for the Messiah

Jesus' healing ministry occupies a large part of the gospels. There are forty-one distinct references to physical and mental healing in the four gospels; in fact, a full one-third of Luke's Gospel focuses on issues of healing.

The ministry of healing was integral to Jesus' understanding of his mission as the Messiah. Very early in his public ministry, he applied the important text of Isaiah 1:1-2 to himself:

> *The Spirit of [God] is upon me,*
> *because [the Most High] has anointed me*
> *   to bring glad tidings to the poor.*
> *[God] has sent me to proclaim liberty to captives*
> *   and recovery of sight to the blind,*
> *   to let the oppressed go free,*
> *and to proclaim a year acceptable to [our God].*

> LUKE 4:18-19

Later, when John's disciples went to inquire about Jesus' identity, they found him curing many people. He told them:

> *Go and tell John what you have seen and heard: the*
> *blind regain their sight, the lame walk, lepers are*

*cleansed, the deaf hear, the dead are raised, the poor
have the good news proclaimed to them.*

By this response, Jesus implied that the healings he
was performing were signs that the Reign of God had
already begun. This Reign will become a full reality as
Jesus ministers in the power of the Spirit of the end times
referred to by the prophet Joel:

*Then afterward
    I will pour out my spirit on all flesh;
your sons and your daughters shall prophesy,
    your old men shall dream dreams,
    and your young men shall see visions.
Even on the male and female slaves,
    in those days, I will pour out my spirit.*

JOEL 2:28-29 (NRSV)

Healing: A Proof of Divinity?

While some scholars conclude that Jesus' healing
ministry was clear proof of his divinity, the gospels do not
emphasize this particular point. Rather, the gospels
emphasize the fact that God, through Christ, came to
bring salvation to all people. The healing power of God,
vibrantly alive in Jesus, liberated people from the bondage of evil and made them whole in mind, heart, body,
and spirit. Rather than focusing on his personal glory and
power, Jesus' healings manifested the divine dimension of
salvation. The exorcisms and healings that Jesus performed offered concrete evidence to support his message
of the dawning Reign of God. They were invitations to
believe in the redemptive power of God present in the
person, message, and actions of Christ. They were not
proofs, but *signs* that called for a decision. Those who
experienced the healing power of Christ could decide

Jesus' Outlook on Healing   9

that he operated in league with Beelzebul, the evil one, or that he embodied the Spirit of God.

Healing: Faith in God Is Required

In the gospels, people are not encouraged to place their faith in Jesus as a miracle worker, but to believe in the power of God present in Christ. This faith would involve an active seeking of God's healing, an energetic grasping after the help of God. When Jesus said, "Your faith has saved you," he implied that the sick person must openly seek God's assistance and that the person's persistence would call forth the power of healing love active in Jesus (Mark 5:34; 10:52). This faith came from the person being cured, from his or her relatives (Mark 7:24-30), or from friends (Mark 2:5; Matthew 8:10).

Although the faith described in the gospel narratives was not directed toward Jesus as a miracle worker, it was linked to his role as the Messiah. It was—and is—through him that the divine power for salvation was—and is—revealed.

In light of the Resurrection, the miracle stories were recorded as clear revelations of the messiahship of Jesus. The messianic titles given to Jesus indicated that he was the one in whom God achieved humankind's redemption and in whom God was directly revealed and was present.

This becomes apparent in studying the way the gospels explain the significance of the healing acts of Jesus. In the synoptic gospels (Mark, Matthew, and Luke) healing acts of Jesus are designated as "acts of power" which, united with his preaching, reinforce Jesus' proclamation of the dawning of the Reign of God. Healings become the Good News in action.

Healing: Conquering the Power of Evil

The gospel writers saw the healings brought about by Jesus as part of his struggle against the power of evil. For

Mark, the cures wrought by Jesus constituted a major assault on the "kingdom" of Satan. If Jesus was to inaugurate the kingdom of God in history, he had to begin by breaking the hold of evil upon the world and liberating people from the control of the devil. Matthew heartily endorsed Mark's view, seeing Jesus' work of healing as an important element in his campaign to destroy Satan's "kingdom" upon earth. In the Gospel of Luke these healing acts signaled the preliminary defeat of evil. Typical of this perspective is the comment of Jesus concerning the cure of the crippled woman: "This daughter of Abraham, whom Satan has bound for eighteen years now, ought she not to have been set free on the sabbath day from this bondage?" (Luke 13:16).

It is important to note that this perspective was based primarily on the biblical understanding that sickness and death were consequences of sin. Human suffering was viewed as a visible sign of the bondage Satan had over the world. Hence, God's primary intention in healing was to destroy the dominion of sin and death, and the power of Satan over all people. Seen in this way, true healing involved the reestablishment of a genuine relationship with God in Christ through the power of the Spirit.

Although some of the gospel stories of healing are linked to people whose suffering was caused by sin, Jesus knew that much human suffering occurs to good people for causes totally unrelated to sinfulness. Jesus expressed a willingness to bring healing in these situations, too. When questioned about the cause of a man's blindness since birth, Jesus replied: "Neither he nor his parents sinned; it is so that the works of God might be made visible through him" (John 9:3).

Healing: A Sign of Salvation

While it is important to emphasize that these healings were an attack on evil and the initial victory over death, they are only a first step toward the final defeat of evil. These healings did not bring a total victory over death. Through his Cross and Resurrection, Jesus Christ brought about the promise of eternal life which begins here and now, but which is only fully revealed on the last day through the resurrection of the dead.

The effects of the Resurrection are not just experienced at the end of the world, however; eternal life begins when we enter into a relationship with Jesus Christ. Jesus is not someone who simply takes away the sicknesses and hurts of our earthly life. Rather, by the power of his Cross and Resurrection, Jesus gives life that endures through suffering and death. Faith in the healing power of Jesus demands a belief in Christ as the one who gives eternal life, the ultimate gift of healing and peace.

To be healed in mind, heart, body, or spirit is more than just a foretaste of the Lord's glory. It is the real thing! To be healed is to be gifted with the "firstfruits of the Spirit" (Romans 8:23). Luke connected Jesus' healings with his future victory. He saw Jesus' acts of power in healing the sick as significant pointers to Jesus' future sovereignty over all oppression, negativity, and evil. Jesus' healing miracles were primarily symbols of that salvation which the Lord would bring to all people.

To comprehend the importance of Jesus' healings, it is necessary to understand that they pointed to the future defeat of the power of evil and death. Both physical and inner healings were genuine signs of that future victory. Just as the biblical authors viewed death as a consequence of sin and a revelation of the power of Satan, they saw healing as pointing to the future Reign of Christ. By conquering death, "the last enemy to be destroyed," Jesus showed that he was the Sovereign One at the right hand of the Father (1 Corinthians 15:26). His sovereignty is not yet complete, however, because his enemies are still alive. The final victory will not come until Jesus comes in glory and "there shall be no more death or mourning, wailing or pain" (Revelation 21:4).

During this present age, each victory over evil, even if it is temporary, is a foreshadowing of the complete victory that is to come. Each physical or inner healing is a sign of the "redemption of our bodies" for which all people patiently wait (Romans 8:23). Seen in this way, healing becomes a genuine symbol of the ultimate salvation of the total person—mind, heart, body, and spirit—which will be experienced fully in the eternal embrace of God in heaven.

Healings: Physical, Spiritual, and Psychological

The gospels witness to a variety of healings: physical, spiritual, and emotional or psychological. Physical healings are the most obvious, even to the casual reader of the New Testament. They often involved a further healing of the person's spirit seen in Jesus' words of forgiveness. Likewise in some of the spiritual healings, Jesus forgave sins and called sinners to a conversion that demanded a total change of heart.

There are many other healings in the gospels that appear to be psychological in nature. This includes some of the presumed exorcisms performed by Jesus, where the Spirit of God appeared to be in direct confrontation with evil spirits. At the time in which the gospels were written, there was no category for mental illness. Neuroses and psychoses as well as some physical illnesses were identified with the powers of evil that originated from unclean spirits. Hence, some of these healings, originally perceived as exorcisms, were quite probably psychological healings in which Christ brought peace and stability to a troubled person.

Healing: Inner Peace Through Christ

While the evangelists seemed to focus on physical and spiritual healings, today we need to direct our attention to the area of inner healing. With all respect to recent psychological research, the development of new terminology, and a heightened awareness of the importance of psychiatric healing, it seems clear that Jesus—two thousand years ago—healed all forms of sickness including emotional and psychological ills.

Jesus was sensitive to how people's self-image and physical well-being were influenced by sin (their own or others). He made a special effort to make a crippled person stand up straight *and* to help that person feel loved and accepted by God. The healing of the paralyzed man let down on a mat through the roof is an example of both inner and physical healing (Luke 5:17-26). Jesus first bestowed inner peace to the person through the forgiveness of sins. This freedom, then, liberated the man so he could be healed of his paralysis and experience the fullness of physical life. Cured of a paralysis that had been both a physical reality and a symptom of his inner bondage, the man went home praising God, demonstrating his internal freedom to praise and witness to the physical healing.

This same sensitivity to people's personal hurts is evidenced in Christ's dealings with two women known for their sinful ways. In the reconciliation of the woman who was a public sinner (Luke 7:36-50) and in the encounter with the Samaritan woman (John 4:1-42), Jesus showed a deep sensitivity to their emotional states as well as to the physical realities of their life situations.

When Jesus told Peter of his coming denial, he said, "I have prayed that your own faith may not fail; and once you have turned back, you must strengthen your brothers [and sisters]" (Luke 22:32). This is a beautiful example of the healing love of God overcoming the shame and guilt that Peter would experience, replacing it with strength that in turn would strengthen the Christian community.

Not everyone accepted Jesus' power to bring healing to heart, mind, body, and spirit. When the Pharisees rejected Jesus and the blind man he had healed, they demonstrated their own blindness and were declared guilty by Jesus who said: "I came into this world for judgment, so that those who do not see might see, and those who do see might become blind....If you were blind, you would have no sin; but now you are saying, 'We see,' so your sin remains" (John 9:39,41).

The consequence of the judgment resulting from Jesus' summons to faith is that some people, like the Pharisees in this story, falsely believed that they already had the light of faith. They did not see their sinfulness, their humanness, their need for healing and wholeness. They rejected Jesus' call to lead a life of repentance, to seek the mercy, forgiveness, and healing of God. If the Pharisees had grasped the reality of their own blindness and need for personal inner healing, there might have been hope that they would search for the light of Christ and accept the power of his healing. Their complacency and unwillingness to change, grow, and admit their human imperfections, however, closed the door to this possibility.

Although each incident of healing in the gospels communicates the triumph of light over darkness, the victory of Christ over the devil, and the power of healing to ease suffering, the story of Jesus healing the blind man is especially significant. The healing of the blind man and the gift of sight for the external world are symbolic of the deeper healing that brings sight and understanding for the inner world. This man's blindness became an occasion for the glory of God to be revealed. The work of God that Jesus accomplished as the Light of the World was—and remains—the work of salvation and healing.

Chapter 3

HEALING *in* THE HISTORY *of* THE CHRISTIAN CHURCH

From the time of the first Christians to the present day, the Church has been conscious of the need to bring healing to its members and to all people in the world. In the early Church, the disciples of Jesus and their successors heeded the Messiah's message and continued to heal the sick (Mark 6:7-13; see also Matthew 10:5-10; Luke 9:1-6). Today, while the importance placed on healing has shifted, the Church continues to respond to Jesus' injunction to bring healing to all.

The healing power of Jesus most definitely flowed through his disciples. When they failed to effect a healing, as in the story of the epileptic demoniac, Jesus made it clear that he expected them to cure the boy. When they asked Jesus to explain why they failed, he instructed them to pray more fervently

(Mark 9:14-29). In this, it appears that Jesus was training his disciples to consider healing as an essential part of their pastoral activity. The early Christian community seems to have adopted the attitude that the followers of Jesus were simply expected to carry on his healing ministry by curing the sick and casting out demons.

Healing in the Acts of the Apostles

Healing appears to have been an essential part of the early Church's ordinary ministry. The Book of the Acts of the Apostles describes the manner in which the disciples carried out this commission. In the name of Jesus, Peter healed the lame man at the gate called Beautiful (Acts 3:6-7), and Paul healed the cripple at Lystra (Acts 14:10). People positioned the sick along the side of the road in such a way that Peter's shadow could fall on them (Acts 5:15). Throughout Acts, we read about people who were cured of a broad range of diseases, including dysentery (Acts 28:8), paralysis (Acts 9:34), and even death (Acts 9:40; 20:10).

Healings also occurred through the ministry of Stephen, Philip, and Ananias of Damascus. The most significant leaders involved in the healing ministry, however, were Peter and Paul. They represented the whole Church and demonstrated that Jesus healed people in and through the Christian community.

While rejoicing in the fact that miracles continued to occur in the Christian community after the Resurrection, we must view miracles within the overall context of Christian ministry and the call to holiness issued to all those who are baptized:

> *Nevertheless, do not rejoice because the spirits are subject to you, but rejoice because your names are written in heaven.*

Luke 10:20

Although the miracles were an essential aspect of Jesus' ministry, the Christian call to holiness always took precedence—and that remains as true for us today as it did for the Christians of the early Church. While healings and miracles are signs of the Lord's power and presence, they do not replace our personal journeys to find healing and peace through daily union with Christ and the Christian community.

Healing in the Writings of Saint Paul

The letters of Paul encouraged Christians to seek a holiness of life based on the imitation of Christ and to share "his sufferings by being conformed to his death" (Philippians 3:10). Although Paul stressed the importance of the Cross and the possibility of suffering in the course of salvation, he did not associate sickness or personal illness with the will of God. He found no inconsistency in healing the sick and alleviating personal pain: "So extraordinary were the mighty deeds God accomplished at the hands of Paul that when face cloths or aprons that touched his skin were applied to the sick, their diseases left them and the evil spirits came out of them" (Acts 19:11-12).

When he spoke of his sufferings for the sake of Christ, Paul did not list physical or emotional illness. Rather, he named the kind of suffering that resulted from persecution and preaching the gospel:

> *I am still more, with far greater labors, far more imprisonments, far worse beatings, and numerous brushes with death. Five times at the hands of the Jews I received forty lashes minus one. Three times I was beaten with rods, once I was stoned, three times I was shipwrecked, I passed a night and a day on the deep.*
> 2 CORINTHIANS 11:23-25

Without diminishing the value of personal suffering for the sake of the gospel, Paul made it clear that he valued physical healing and recognized the importance of inner healing in the process of spiritual growth. Addressing this topic in his letter to the church at Ephesus, Paul pointed out the need for the "hidden self" to grow strong in the Spirit. He noted that it was through this inner self that Christ lived in people's hearts, and that by living in communion with their inner selves they could lead lives of love and thus be "filled with all the fullness of God" (Ephesians 3:19).

The Letter to the Colossians carried this a step further, pointing out that inner healing led to a deeper union with Christ that enabled Christians to reflect the glory of God in the world (Colossians 3:10). This observation also reflected the reality that this inner re-creation did not happen instantly, but occurred as part of a process in which there was a deep integration of the intellect, emotions, will, and body.

Paul's understanding of the relationship between the psychological dimension and the spiritual dimension of the human person is clear in the Letter to the Ephesians:

> *Be renewed in the spirit of your minds, and put on the new self, created in God's way in righteousness and holiness of truth.*
>
> EPHESIANS 4:23-24

In this, Paul indicated that the psychological dimension of a person's being could only be renewed by the spiritual. With this insight Paul provided a timeless understanding of healing and the human person: true self-knowledge and inner healing of emotional wounds often come through spiritual means. As this happens in the lives of individuals, they discover their true selves as holy and centered in God, no longer living according to painful illusions.

Healing in the Early Centuries

Prayer for physical and inner healing was a common experience among the group of scholars, writers, Church leaders, and saints who lived in the first centuries after Christ. Irenaeus (born in Asia Minor around the year 130 A.D.) testified to a wide variety of healings during his lifetime. In his treatise, *Against Heresies,* an identifying mark of the heretic was the fact that he or she was not able to perform the miracles of healing that Christians accomplished. A heretic did not possess the power of God and thus lacked the power to bring healing. Among believers, on the other hand, Irenaeus witnessed to all types of healing. He saw healing as a natural activity of Christians that channels the creative power of God through prayer:

> *For they are able to give sight to the blind, hearing to the deaf, to put all demons to flight....The infirm, or the lame, or those paralysed, or those disturbed in other parts of the body, are cured; it often happens that those who have contracted some bodily illness or have had some kind of accident, are restored in this way to good.*

Origen, another scholar of the early Church, related how Christians "expel evil spirits and perform many cures" (*Against Celsus*). In his explanation of the effects of healing prayer, he stated that "the name of Jesus can still remove distractions from the minds of men and expel demons, and also take away diseases." Origen believed the name of Jesus could cause a total healing in a person's life. He cited examples in which the gift of healing was also shared by the Greeks and barbarians who accepted Jesus Christ and who invoked the name of Jesus in prayer:

*For by these means, we too have seen many persons
freed from grievous calamities, and from distractions of
mind, and madness, and countless other ills....*

During these early years of the Church's life, the
Christian community was also known for its ability to
bring healing to the mentally ill or "demon-possessed." In
fact, people came to the Church seeking relief so frequently
that exorcism became a regular part of the Church's ritual
life. Of the methods employed to effect this healing, one
rebuked the evil spirit in the name of Jesus. Other methods
involved laying hands on, touching, or breathing on the
mentally ill person. Sometimes during the ceremony,
accounts of Jesus' healing actions were related and holy
water was utilized.

The desert mothers who lived in the fifth-century
Egyptian desert have left us a rich legacy on inner healing
prayer. They saw the Christian life as a journey toward
holiness and wholeness in body-mind-spirit. An example
of this is the following story by Amma (Mother)
Theodora. "There was in fact, a nun who was seized by
cold and fever every time she began to pray, and she
suffered from headaches, too. In this condition she said to
herself, 'I am ill, and near death, so now I will get up
before I die and pray.' By reasoning in this way, she did
violence to herself and prayed. When she had finished,
the fever abated also. So by reasoning in this way, the
sister resisted, and prayed and was able to conquer her
thoughts..." (cited in Barbara Bowe, et al, *Silent Voices,
Sacred Lives*, Paulist, 1992).

Healing in the Time of Saint Augustine

Saint Augustine (354-430), a convert and a bishop, is
recognized as one of the major shapers of Christian
theology. Many of his ideas still form the basis for contemporary formulations of Christian beliefs.

Amid Augustine's many written works and published sermons are his thoughts on miracles and healing. In his early writings he stated clearly that Christians are not to seek the gift of healing. His perspective changed, however, and he later admitted that he had been wrong. In one of the final sections of *The City of God*, he described miracles of healing that occurred in his own diocese of Hippo in northern Africa:

> *I realized how many miracles were occurring in our own day and which were so like the miracles of old and also how wrong it would be to allow the memory of these marvels of divine power to perish from among our people. It is only two years ago that the keeping of records was begun here in Hippo, and already, at this writing, we have nearly seventy attested miracles.*
>
> Book XXII, Chapter 8

In Augustine's thinking, the world is sustained by the immanent power of God. When humankind began to take this marvelous reality of grace for granted, however, God broke through in a more unusual manner, using healings and miracles to draw people's attention to God's presence in the world.

In his book, *Confessions*, Augustine told of his conversion to Christianity and offered an example of Healing-of-Memories Prayer. He related several incidents that touched his life deeply. As he wrote about each event, he shared his thoughts, feelings, and prayerful reflections, describing how God utilized each situation—joyful and painful—as an opportunity for grace and healing.

Healing in the Middle Ages

We cannot overemphasize the influence of Gregory the Great, Bishop of Rome from 590 to 604 A.D., in formulating the medieval approach to miracles and healing. Gregory saw miracles of healing as a foretaste of heaven and as the perfect union of humankind with God that we would experience there. His view of how healing helped people draw closer to God also presented people with a clearer vision of the purpose of their lives: total union with God, peace with other people, and complete harmony with all creation. This capacity to look at reality in its totality as being re-created by God led Gregory to view miracles as signs of the last age. In his view, miraculous healings pointed toward the conclusion of time, making the world the "antechamber of heaven." He included the power of the saints in his approach to healing and urged people to see how they had "friends at court" who would intercede for them in their needs and difficulties.

From this perspective, the healing miracles that occurred through the intercession of the saints revealed heaven to people on earth. This familiarity with the saints—and the growing desire to be in close contact with them by visiting the places where their bodies were buried—created the great shrines and pilgrimage routes of the Middle Ages.

This effort to find healing of mind, heart, body, and spirit through the saints and especially through Mary has not abated. Christians of every tradition make pilgrimages to shrines and seek healing through the prayer of the saints, especially Mary, the mother of Jesus.

Healing in an Era of Decline

Although miracles in the Middle Ages have their moments of greatness, they do not appear to be as impressive as the spiritual accounts described by Irenaeus, Origen, Augustine, and Gregory. For example, Thomas Aquinas (1225-1274), one of the most influential theologians of all times, did not address the question of religious healing except as it occurred during the lifetime of the apostles. In Part III of the *Summa Theologica*, Aquinas stated that the purpose of these early Christian healing miracles was to prove Christ's teaching and to demonstrate his divinity. He observed that Christ came especially for the salvation of our souls, and that it was proper for Christ to manifest the power to heal. Aquinas did not readily see others bringing healing as Christ did.

While it was "fitting that Christ, by miraculously healing people, should prove himself to be the universal and spiritual Savior of all," Aquinas clearly focused more attention on the soul:

> *The soul is more important than the body….By how much a soul is of more account than a body, by so much is the forgiving of sins a greater work than healing the body; but because the one is unseen [God] does the lesser and more manifest thing in order to prove the greater and more unseen.*

III.44.3, AD. 1 AND 3

Aquinas taught that the saints performed miracles, not so much out of compassion for human suffering as to foster knowledge of salvation.

Thomas Aquinas, revered as the foremost Catholic theologian of all ages, was not the only person to question the validity of healing miracles. Martin Luther, often called the "father of the Reformation," also believed that miracles occurred in the early centuries but people then moved beyond healing miracles by spiritually teaching and converting humankind.

Luther's attitude greatly influenced Protestant thought and practices regarding healing. He emphasized faith, prayer, love, and the sacraments of baptism and Eucharist over miracles and healing. Private confession was encouraged insofar as it led the believer to spiritual health. Recognizing that many physical sicknesses had their origin in spiritual anxiety, guilt, fear, and temptation, Luther encouraged people to seek help through prayer and spiritual guidance. In addition, he saw the therapeutic value of forgiveness and love in interpersonal relationships.

John Calvin, another Reformer, also believed that miracles were only a temporary phenomena present in the early centuries of the Church. He felt that they were needed at the beginning of Christianity because they would enhance the preaching of the gospel.

Calvin's doctrine of providence also influenced his attitude toward sickness and healing. According to this teaching, everything that occurred in a person's life was ordained by God. Hence, this belief fostered a general attitude of resignation to sickness as the will of God. People did not pray for healing, expect a miracle, or even try to overcome their illnesses when this mind set prevailed.

As a general rule, the Reformers rejected the belief in the effectiveness of relics and shrines, and focused their attention on the prayer of faith, confession to God, and the spiritual guidance of the pastor as the most important elements for the health of the believer.

The Catholic Reformers attempted to rid the Catholic Church of the abuses that led to the Reformation, and to respond with zeal against the teachings of the Reformers. While there was an effort to clarify and present Catholic teaching about the intercession of the saints and the value of prayer, there was still a hesitancy among many Catholics to expect that God could or would work healing miracles in their lives. The thinking of Thomas Aquinas was not easily refuted, and yet there were people who did see a place for healing miracles in the sixteenth-century Church.

Healing in the Lives of Saints

One of the most prominent spiritual leaders of the Church in the era of the Counter-Reformation was Saint Philip Neri, born in Florence, Italy, in 1515. Neri founded a new religious community called the Oratorians, whose major work was to care for the stranger and the sick. Working with his community, Saint Philip became involved in a major healing ministry. His approach consisted of prayer for healing, laying on of hands, and fostering an attitude of expectant faith in his ability to bring healing. The story is told of a woman with cancer of the breast. Before the doctor was able to apply a hot iron to cauterize the cancer, Philip touched the cancer, prayed with the woman for healing, and assured her that she would recover. When the doctor came to cauterize the cancer, he was surprised to discover the woman completely healed.

The prayer of Clare of Assisi (1195-1253), foundress of the Poorhadies, (popularly known as the Poor Clares), healed epilepsy, leprosy, and many other diseases. According to one story, she prevented an attack on her home town—Assisi. Clare placed ashes on her head and on the heads of her sisters. Then all went to pray in the chapel. The next day the army departed the city peacefully (Carol L. Flinders, *Enduring Grace*, Harper San Francisco, 1993).

Francis Xavier, a personal friend of Ignatius Loyola, the founder of the Jesuits, is well known for his missionary endeavors in India, Japan, China, and the East Indies. Like others of his time, he relied on the usual medical practices to fight disease, but he is also credited with a number of miraculous healings. The story is told of a four-year-old child who had been sick with a high fever for several months. When Francis placed his hand upon the dying child's forehead, read a passage of Scripture, offered a prayer, and made the Sign of the

Cross, the child opened his eyes, smiled, and began an immediate recovery.

Healing in the Modern Era

The gift of healing has played a significant role throughout the history of the Church, especially among individuals working to comfort the poor and the sick. Despite the cautions issued by scholars and writers against hoping or praying or working for healing miracles, those interested in relieving the suffering of their fellow human beings turn to prayer.

In addition to the prominent people already mentioned, one could look at the ministries of healing exercised by Vincent de Paul, Louise de Marillac, Saint Terese Lisieux, Catherine of Sienna, and many other recent saints and holy people. Although they might be better remembered for other achievements, healing was a major part of their ministry.

While scholars and Church leaders continue to question the authenticity of healing miracles, people of genuine faith continue to seek healing at the shrines of Mary and the saints. They place great faith in novenas, relics, and special prayers, and more often than not their faith is rewarded with a renewed sense of well-being, peace, and oneness with God.

Since the late 1960s there has been a greater willingness on the part of many Christians to believe that the power of Jesus to heal is present in the Church through the workings of the Holy Spirit. As men and women, ordained and unordained, exercise Spirit-filled ministries of healing, the gift of healing remains present in the Church, as it was in the days of the apostles. This increased awareness of the possibilities of healing challenges us to study, understand, appreciate, and celebrate the role of healing in the context of Christian life, prayer, holiness, and salvation.

Chapter 4

PAIN *and* SUFFERING, HEALING *and* SALVATION

The relationship between pain and suffering, and healing and salvation as reflected in the Bible, the life of Christ, and the traditions and teachings of the Church greatly influences contemporary outlooks toward these issues. Current Church practices are shaped by Jesus' perspective on the relationship between healing and salvation, the actions of saints, and the decisions of ecclesial bodies.

Healing and Salvation

In his preaching and in his actions, Jesus was careful to link individual healing miracles with his more general mission of bringing salvation to all people. He also made it clear that the apostles and their successors were to establish the bond between healing and salvation. Jesus intended the visible signs of healing to be symbolic of the not-as-visible signs of salvation.

The Church as the living Body of Christ participates in Christ's struggle against evil and furthers his desire to bring salvation, healing, and freedom, as well as victory over sin and death, pain and suffering. The healings that occur through the prayers and rituals of the Church are signs of the victory that Jesus has already gained over death by his Cross and Resurrection. They are also indicative of the final victory in which the Church will share when "the last enemy to be destroyed is death" (1 Corinthians 15:26). Healing becomes a clear sign of the kingdom based on the redemptive mystery of the Cross and Resurrection of Jesus Christ.

Although the healing of sickness can be a sign of salvation, it is not essential that everyone who is saved also be healed of any or all physical or emotional sicknesses. Healing is a sign of the "redemption of our bodies" (Romans 8:23), but it does not mean that this redemption has been fully achieved. Nor does it mean that without visible healing there is no redemption. Still, healing is an important sign of the tremendous reality of salvation, although it is not experienced in every situation.

Healing Versus Salvation

Scripture presents an apparent paradox. On the one hand, Jesus told his followers to carry their crosses; yet, whenever he encountered individuals who were sick, he healed them. Jesus' actions and message, however, are not as contradictory as they might first appear.

In his book, *Healing* (Ave Maria Press, 1974), Francis MacNutt makes a helpful distinction between two different types of suffering:

The suffering that Jesus bore was the anguish of persecution, the type of suffering that comes from outside a person because of the misunderstanding of others. For example, Jesus warns his followers that

they will be persecuted, and thrown in jail, that their
enemies will be their own brothers and sisters, and that
they are to be happy when these evil things occur
(Matthew 10:16-33). Likewise, Jesus suffered inner
pain but the source of his suffering was outside himself.
Jesus struggled with fear in the Garden of Geth-
semane; he was mocked, scourged, nailed to a cross,
and died. However, Jesus did not suffer from physical
or emotional sickness that is destructive to the well-
being of the human person. Rather, this was the type of
suffering that he removed from those who came to him
in faith (78).

This twofold distinction is obvious in the life of Jesus. Although the Pharisees, high priests, and high-ranking officials responded to his preaching and healing ministry with insults, rejection, and the death penalty, there is no mention in the gospels of Jesus being physically or emotionally sick. Nowhere do we find any evidence that Jesus suffered from any of the diseases, physical or emotional, that were prevalent in his time. Thus, it seems safe to conclude that Jesus was an emotionally and physically healthy person and that his sufferings were from external causes.

Healing and Redemptive Suffering

That God desires us to be healed of physical and emotional sickness does not mean that we endorse an attitude that neglects suffering or omits the Cross. The gospel preached by Christ and his followers looks on physical and psychological sickness as an evil to be eradicated when it damages the quality of life. Suffering endured for the Reign of God, suffering that entails transforming and liberating oppressive structures, is to be endured courageously for the sake of the gospel, not for its own sake.

If God is revealed through the words and actions of Jesus—which clearly favor health in mind, heart, body, and spirit—it is safe to conclude that God wants us to be whole rather than emotionally or physically ill. What's more, God does not want us to suffer from the evil actions of others. But we do suffer—and when we do, we often turn to God with prayers for healing. In countless ways, God often responds. There are times when God does not heal, however, because of blockages put in the way or because the illness serves a higher purpose or effects a deeper union of the person with God.

Healing and suffering are not mutually exclusive. A treatise on healing that ignores the important value of suffering is not in accord with the gospel of Jesus Christ. Likewise, a theology of redemptive suffering that neglects to mention divine healing power contradicts the Good News preached by Jesus. Throughout the history of the Church, and especially in the first half of the twentieth century, the focus has been placed on redemptive suffering without specific recognition of the healing power of the Spirit present in prayer, individuals, and the Christian community. In more recent times the emphasis has been placed on the healing power of the Spirit in the Church.

Healing and the Value of Suffering

Suffering accepted in union with Christ fosters both personal growth in holiness and a union with Christ's suffering that has value for the salvation of the whole world. It is important, however, to distinguish between suffering which God redeems by comforting, healing, and strengthening individuals, and suffering which God uses to further the sacred purpose of reconciling the world. Both are related to the mystery of union with Christ in his suffering.

In suffering where Christ brings redemptive healing, we experience the presence of Christ's redemptive love in the midst of pain and healing. Suffering becomes joy, and God is praised for the gift of healing, a visible manifestation of the Resurrection.

Through suffering which is not readily healed or alleviated but which God makes redemptive, we participate in the saving work of Christ by offering our sufferings in union with Christ for the salvation of the whole world. Through the power of the Cross and Resurrection of Jesus Christ, divine life flows into life, and Jesus bestows the power to cooperate with him by participating in his reconciling and healing ministry:

> *Creation was made subject to futility, not of its own accord but because of the one who subjected it, in hope that creation itself would be set free from slavery to corruption and share in the glorious freedom of the children of God.*
>
> ROMANS 8:20-21

There is no contradiction between offering suffering, sickness, and anxiety for personal spiritual development and the salvation of the world, and at the same time praying for healing. Paul reflects on the meaning of redemptive suffering:

> *[God] encourages us in our every affliction, so that we may be able to encourage those who are in any affliction with the encouragement with which we ourselves are encouraged by God. For as sufferings overflow to us, so through Christ does our encouragement also overflow. If we are afflicted, it is for your encouragement and salvation; if we are encouraged, it is for your encouragement, which enables you to endure the same sufferings that we suffer.*
>
> 2 CORINTHIANS 1:4-6

When we unite our sufferings with those of Christ, we participate in the eternal sacrifice for the salvation of all men and women. God uses our human sufferings to promote the reconciling the world. Thus, suffering in union with Christ becomes a powerful form of intercessory prayer and a source of blessing and consolation for the entire Body of Christ.

When we pray for healing with other people, we share with them the good news of God's healing power. As ministers of God's healing love, we become channels of divine compassion, open to whatever Jesus may do. Sometimes we will experience complete healing; sometimes we may discover a deep peace and a new acceptance of a difficult situation or relationship; sometimes we may block or reject God's healing.

To minister to people who are in pain, we must be messengers of hope—hope for physical and inner healing through the power of the Cross and Resurrection of Jesus Christ, and hope for the salvation of the world through redemptive suffering in union with the Cross and Resurrection of Jesus Christ.

Healing and the Kingdom

Keep in mind that the healings of Jesus were signs of the coming of the Reign of God. While he did not remove all physical and emotional illness from human experience, Jesus did heal the sick people who approached him during his earthly ministry. Following his lead, the disciples continued to proclaim the gospel message throughout the world and accompanied their preaching with signs of Christ's power over evil, including the healing of the sick and the raising of the dead. The apostles, like Christ, did not remove all illness or suffering from humankind.

To understand why Christ, the apostles, or today's ministers of healing do not bring healing to all people, it is helpful to see healing as a sign of the victory over death that has begun but that is not yet complete. Each healing is a gift that points toward the redemption of the body for which all Christians wait with eager hearts. Since we are still subject to death and suffering, however, we cannot demand to be liberated from the sources of death, such as sickness and pain. Healing is a foretaste of the resurrection of the body, which God freely grants as a sign of Christ's victory over death. God's freedom to perform such signs is beyond human comprehension. There is no way to know or understand why some people are healed through prayer while others remain ill.

While being healed of sickness through prayer is a type of victory over death, the acceptance of illness can also be a victory of God's grace and the human spirit over the power of destruction and death. Although sickness can be seen as something evil and a consequence of original sin, accepting illness as part of God's plan for salvation can bring about genuine inner healing. Countless stories are told of people who travel to places such as Lourdes or Fatima in hope of physical healing, to return home with great peace and joy—but no physical healing. Their journey, however, left them with a·profound sense of God's redemptive plan so that they were better able to experience meaning in their sickness.

Healing and Growth Through Suffering

Physical or emotional illness can be part of God's plan. Sometimes it challenges our complacency in matters of religion and restores our priorities in life. Sometimes sickness, suffering, or pain causes us to change our direction in life so that God may truly be the focus of all human endeavors. Such a change of heart can be seen in the apostle Paul who was blinded en route to Damascus and, as a result of this misfortune, discovered that the Lord called him to a radical conversion—a total change of direction. His blindness lasted three days, until

Ananias laid his hands upon him and healed him (Acts 9:1-19).

Suffering can also teach us a lesson and challenge us to grow and change. For instance, those of us who suffer headaches, irritability, and excessive tension from daily stress might examine our pain and find that our sense of self-worth has been severely diminished from years of trying to do for others and gain their approval. A similar series of sufferings can arise from a perfectionist attitude that demands total perfection from self and others. Attitudes like these create a distorted perspective that causes much unhappiness and strain. This inner pain cannot be healed until we confront the causes of the stress and take action to remedy the situation. Until we have examined our pain and discovered its source, prayers for inner healing will be of little benefit.

Pain can be a teacher that helps us trace sufferings to their source so that the cause of the pain can be seen before we pray for inner healing. Different approaches to praying for inner healing, helpful as they may be, are not "quick fixes" for those areas of inner pain that need deeper reflection and immediate action before healing can occur. First we need to recognize the lessons of inner discomfort, hurt, and stress, and take responsibility for changing our lives. Only then, when we are more in harmony with the ways of God, are we ready for inner healing prayer.

Suffering and inner woundedness also remind us that we are pilgrims on a journey to eternity. This world is not a lasting home; pain reminds us that we are still on the way to our eternal home. No amount of prayer for physical or inner healing will be able to alleviate all our emptiness and struggle; the Cross is a reality in every Christian's journey. Sometimes it is only when inner hurts tear away all human pretenses of self-sufficiency and strip us of all our defenses that we recognize our true dependence on God. In this way suffering can become an instrument of God's transforming love, drawing us closer to the Holy One in our midst through greater awareness of God's power and presence.

One of the central truths of the Christian faith is that God gives us peace and joy and is present to us in the midst of frustration, suffering, and inner pain. The struggle and pain endured in this life need not destroy our faith in the reality of God's presence. God is most clearly present not in spite of our human difficulties but because of them. God's compassionate presence often speaks most powerfully in the upsetting and lonely moments of life. There God is discovered, loving us amid our worst fears, anxieties, and pain. In all that is hurtful, we can discover something that is creative and that can help us be conscious of the glory of God hidden within pain. Through an encounter with suffering we can often discover the deep meaning of God's healing and redeeming love.

Healing of the Total Person

Many of us find it hard to believe that healing of minds, hearts, bodies, and spirits is possible. A lack of faith makes us fearful about praying for healing and skeptical about reports of healings taking place in the Christian community today. Some of this fear is due to the fact that until recent times many theologians and spiritual writers discounted the possibility of miraculous healings. They suggested that human beings were meant to suffer in this life, and that carrying our own cross in imitation of Jesus would reap rich heavenly rewards.

The contemporary emphasis on healing, however, stems from a broader and deeper understanding of the Resurrection as the central mystery of redemption. The Spirit dwelling in the People of God, the Body of Christ, is empowering us to live more fully the victory of Jesus.

Coupled with this emphasis on the importance of the Resurrection is a clearer understanding of healing for the whole person and a new awareness of the importance of the resurrected life in the spiritual journey. It is clear that even now Jesus is liberating us from the consequences of original sin. Our Savior frees us from ignorance, from disoriented emotions, and from physical sickness to provide us with a new relationship of intimacy with the Creator through the power of the Holy Spirit.

Christ invites us to enter into a profound union of healing and harmony with God through the power of the Spirit. He promised: "I came so that they might have life and have it more abundantly" (John 10:10). This is the good news of the gospel. We need to learn this good news about healing and allow the saving power of Christ's healing love to permeate our entire existence and transform our lives, for healing is the logical consequence of the gospel message of salvation which proclaims that Jesus came to free us from sin and physical and emotional illness. With that freedom, we can be his witnesses by our loving service to others.

The Resurrection of Jesus anticipates the inauguration of the world to come. In his risen state, Jesus transcends all time and space; the Christ of faith is present always and everywhere, in women and men of all races, cultures, and creeds. Because the Risen One embraces the ultimate future and all that it encompasses, Christ holds the future of the universe and the future of each human person in loving hands. In light of this, we are called not only to recognize the sovereignty of Jesus Christ over the entire universe but also to recognize Jesus as a personal savior who gives meaning to everyday life. Just as all of creation discovers its true meaning and fulfillment in the risen Christ, so each of us can discover our own deepest personal fulfillment through the power of the Spirit dwelling within.

The risen Christ is actively present in our own personal history, giving us value and lending meaning to life. Just as God's plan from the beginning of existence has been to reconcile and unify everything in Christ, so too God's plan is to reconcile, heal, and unify everything in the life of each of us through the power of the Spirit. While this process will take a lifetime and will only be completed in eternity, it begins today with the healing of mind, heart, body, and spirit. The possibility of healing tempered by the reality that final union with Christ comes only in eternity gives reason to hope for healing and yet to be patient with the profound process of ongoing healing and transformation in Christ.

Chapter 5

THE NEED
for HEALING
TODAY

In a world filled with woundedness, suffering, and pain there is an urgent need for healing in many different forms. In the quest for healing, we must come to realize that the ultimate source of our healing is Christ. Christian healing is the visible manifestation of the salvation brought by the Cross and Resurrection of Christ. It involves both the immediacy of miraculous healing and the ongoing and seemingly more routine deepening of our relationship with God.

Jesus referred to salvation as the living out of a relationship with him: "I am the way and the truth and the life. No one comes to the Father except through me" (John 14:6). The healing of woundedness begins as we experience Christ as an intimate friend, partner, companion, and lover.

The image of friendship accurately describes what happens in inner healing prayer. Faithfully and prayerfully we share our story as openly as possible with Jesus, allowing our

Healer to offer silent support of affirmation, and to send the wisdom of the Spirit. As Christ's loving presence enters our suffering with a physical illness or a complex situation or a difficult relationship, the pain no longer has the power to inflict great damage for "the truth will set you free" (John 8:32).

Praying for Inner Healing

Inner healing includes a method of praying, either alone or with another, in which we ask God to join our pain to Christ's own suffering on the cross. In return God gives us the grace to find our true self, centered in Christ, so that we can love and serve others with new freedom and generosity.

Inner healing has two parts: faithful prayer, and living authentic lives of love and service. While God is the only one who can bring healing, we must respond by accepting healing and being willing to change our lives. In inner healing we allow Christ to liberate us from bondage, open us to his healing love for past sufferings, and choose to bring his presence to the world.

According to Thomas Dobson in his article "Personal Healing Through Prayer" (*Chicago Studies*, November, 1984, p. 301), inner healing can be viewed as having two phases. First, there is remedial healing when a person examines the wounds of the past and changes his or her perspective about them so that they do not have a destructive influence on the present. Second, there is the progressive healing phase in which present day issues are examined so that the person may experience growth in love of God and others, and can express this in an increased capacity to unite every relationship, emotion, thought, and feeling to Christ.

Inner healing prayer starts when we approach God with openness, exposing our neediness and woundedness to God's healing love. Under the influence of healing light, the broken areas of life can be made whole. Inner healing prayer brings us into a right relationship with God, with other people, and with all of creation. Inner healing is discovered in approaching God each day, admitting our needs, and trusting that "everything is possible to one who has faith" (Mark 9:23). Inner healing is discovered when God's healing love is allowed to touch the painful areas of life, knowing that:

> A bruised reed [God] shall not break,
> and a smoldering wick [God] shall not quench.
>
> ISAIAH 42:3

Inner healing prayer provides a way to experience redemption on a day-to-day basis. As we discover our inner woundedness and the areas of bondage in our lives, we need to experience the power of the Cross and Resurrection of Christ saving and healing us on a daily basis. Healing prayer, which has been part of the Christian heritage from the days of the apostles, is one way in which the liberating power of God assists us in resolving conflicts and experiencing a new freedom and wholeness in our spiritual journey.

Helping People Find Healing

All Christians may be used by God as channels of healing love. The Letter of James reminds us to "pray for one another, that you may be healed" (5:16). This message is addressed to all Christians and assures us that God's healing power is present when we pray; the ministry of inner healing prayer is not limited to a few professional faith healers (priests, deacons, prayer-group leaders). All Christians should pray for their own healing and for the healing of people around them. Each of us is called to be an instrument of God's love to those who cross our paths in need of healing. Healing prayer begins, of course, by praying for the healing of those who are closest and dearest to us. A true Christian response to all those who are hurting is: "I love you and want to pray with you."

When we engage in healing prayer we should mirror God's love which is tender, compassionate, and caring. We simply cannot offer healing prayers and remain cold or distant in our feelings, attitudes, or behavior toward the people for whom and with whom we pray. We must adopt Christ's attitude and become personally involved with the people in need of healing by talking with them, finding out why they are hurting, touching them gently, and speaking healing words which set them free and make them whole.

Becoming Instruments of Healing

As instruments of inner healing, we are called to do more than pray for others. First, we have to listen with sensitivity to the pain of other people. The love of Christ becomes incarnate as we listen to people who are hurting, affirm their basic goodness as unique images of God, and permit them to express their feelings about the illnesses, situations, or relationships that burden them. When we express genuine concern for those who are hurting and assist them in discovering the healing power of God in the midst of the painful areas of their lives, we affirm them and help them to be more open to the inner healing process. People who are affirmed by at least one caring person are more willing to deal with the painful areas in their lives.

Second, it is important for us to pray for ourselves as ministers of healing, that we might be open to the inspirations of the Spirit so that we can discern the areas of a person's life that are in need of healing. As healers, we must listen to the Spirit to understand God's love and plan for the person in need. We need to ask the Lord to show us how to pray for healing in a particular set of circumstances. We need to adopt God's vision and speak loving words of consolation and wisdom.

Third, we especially need to be sensitive to the fear, guilt, shyness, and anxiety that hide within people who are hurting. The process of healing will be hastened when we listen to people speak about their feelings in an open, receptive way, and offer them a message of hope. At the same time, we must help them to see that their feelings are not the only reality in the situation they face. We must help them adopt the balanced vision marked by faith and confidence in the power of God.

Fourth, we should pray with faith. "Faith is the realization of what is hoped for and evidence of things not seen" (Hebrews 11:1). Since faith is first of all a gift, we should pray that we and the person in need of healing will be blessed with this gift. While there are many instances where Jesus' faith in the power of God effected the healing, the gospels record several instances where the faith of the recipient was instrumental in the healing. When the woman touched the hem of his garment, Jesus said that the woman's faith had healed her (Matthew 9:20-22). The faith of others also can play a role in healing. The faith of the paralytic's companions can be a model for those of us today who intercede on behalf of friends in need of healing (Mark 2:1-12).

Finally, it is good to remember that healing is a process that happens in God's time and according to divine plan. Those of us seeking healing and praying with others for healing need to be open to the will of God and to pray with faith and compassionate hearts. As ministers of inner healing, we are instruments of God's healing love.

PART TWO

TEN WAYS TO
PRAY FOR HEALING

HEALING-*of*-MEMORIES PRAYER

We view our lives through the perspective of our memories. Memories influence all that we think and say and do. Our relationships, thoughts, feelings, and plans are enhanced or limited by the way we view ourselves. When our memories are positive, we tend to see ourselves as loved and capable of loving, gifted, free, and secure. When our memories are negative, we tend to see ourselves as unlovable and unloving, weak, dependent, and insecure.

Healing-of-Memories Prayer can change the structure of our remembered experience so that we can be freed and healed of past hurts. In this form of prayer we open ourselves to the power of Jesus so he can heal the memory of a painful event or relationship. We allow the Lord to transform that which was wounded into a more peaceful memory.

Healing-of-Memories Prayer focuses on one memory or event in our lives that has caused us pain. Using the gift of faith in an imaginative way, we "turn and become like children" so that we can enter the Reign of God (Matthew 18:3). We do not "invent" the presence of Christ or manipulate images to produce desired results; rather, this style of prayer, if used with trust and openness, has a life of its own that cannot be controlled. We let the gift of healing wash away our painful past.

In this prayer style we use our memories and our faith to discover how Jesus actually interacted with us and with others involved in our painful memories. Because Jesus is the one who always loves us, his words and actions give us the healing and strength we needed but didn't receive or couldn't realize at the time. As we see Jesus and listen to him in the midst of the memory or event from our past, we have a chance to receive his healing love. What had been painful then becomes a moment of grace as Jesus reveals his love to us within the memory.

Healing-of-Memories Prayer, for example, helped a woman who could not develop close relationships with men. Relying on this prayer, which exercised her imagination and faith, she discovered the source of her pain and fear. As a child she experienced lengthy separations from her father due to military assignments. She dreaded the good-byes and worried constantly that each good-bye might be the last.

Using the healing-of-memories approach in her prayer for healing, the woman invited Jesus into one of her most painful childhood memories. She imagined herself as a five-year-old child standing in a hot, crowded airport, wearing her favorite yellow dress, choking back tears, and kissing her father good-bye. She recalled the desperate loneliness she experienced as her father's plane took off—and the waves of fear that something horrible might happen to him before he returned.

In her prayer the woman poured out all the negative feelings that filled her heart: anger, fear, loneliness. As she shared her pain with Jesus, she began to sense that God's protective presence was with her at that moment long ago when she felt most alone. In the present moment, she experienced the loving care of God that surrounded her and her father at the airport years ago. Suddenly she realized that God loved her father far more than she did, and that God had taken care of him—and always would. She also felt secure in the knowledge that God loved her—then and now. For the first time in years this woman felt a sense of joy. She realized that God had always been with her in all the events and relationships of her life.

In the weeks that followed this prayer experience, the woman discovered a greater openness to the gift of friendship and love in herself. She no longer feared abandonment by God or by the important people in her life. In a spirit of confidence and trust, she sought new friendships.

A married couple experiencing difficulty in their relationship also found help through Healing-of-Memories Prayer. Although they had seen a counselor, worked on communication skills, and were well versed in conflict resolution, nothing seemed to work. They were held captive by past resentments and grudges that paralyzed them. While continuing with their own efforts, they also turned to healing prayer.

In their prayer the couple invited Christ to be with them as they reviewed some painful events in their married life. Through their prayer they were able to acknowledge their individual weaknesses, forgive each other for past failures, and communicate more openly. In the months that followed they continued to use this prayer approach whenever old hostilities resurfaced. As a result they discovered a whole new phase of growth in their relationship.

In the gospel we encounter Christ as the healer of negative memories and hurtful experiences. The disciples, on the road to Emmaus, shared their loneliness and discussed how the crucifixion and death of Jesus had destroyed all their hopes and dreams for the kingdom of God. Walking with them as they sadly poured out their feelings of loss, the stranger listened. Then, in the breaking of the bread, Christ revealed his healing presence, transformed their memories and their lives, and filled them with burning love and radiant joy (Luke 24:13-35).

Understanding Healing-of-Memories Prayer

Like these early disciples, and like the woman and the married couple, begin your healing process by sharing painful emotions, past failures, and hurtful memories with Christ. The first steps in the healing process are to recognize personal emotions such as anger, fear, jealousy, resentment, or guilt, accept these feelings, and investigate their source in your memories. You can often trace the reason for negative feelings or behavior patterns to a painful memory that needs healing. You may need to forgive a parent for abuse or neglect. You may have come from a dysfunctional home in which several generations suffered the damaging effects of negative memories. You may, in fact, need to travel back in time to incidents involving deceased members of your family.

Many present day hurts can be found in adult children of alcoholics who have carried the emotional scars of their parents' alcoholism into their own adult lives. If you find yourself in this situation, pray for forgiveness and healing for all family members, past and present, who have suffered from the negative effects of alcoholism.

Many alcoholics, drug addicts, and others with addictive disorders have discovered that it is absolutely essential in the recovery process to replace negative thought patterns with positive affirmations. Healing-of-Memories Prayer is one effective way to accomplish this goal. Each time a negative thought or image surfaces, simply release it to Christ, and ask him to replace it with a new positive image of his healing love. This process is enriched when you actually visualize the letting go of the negative thought or image, allowing Christ to fill the emptiness with a positive image or affirmation of his healing, vibrant love. Since incorporating this healthy way of thinking and living into daily life usually happens over a period of time and requires constant effort, an effective support system such as Alcoholics Anonymous, Overeaters Anonymous, or Al-Anon is essential.

Once you discover the source of your suffering, you can share that particular painful memory or relationship with Christ, remembering that he suffered, died, and rose from the dead so that all life's broken situations can be healed. Because of the redemptive power of Christ's death and resurrection, pain can become a source of spiritual growth. Memories of failure, sin, and weakness can be transformed into occasions of growth. The images of past sins can be cleansed, and you can be delivered from bondage to evil, thereby becoming free to relate more intimately with Christ.

Although Christ can heal a memory the first time we pray for healing, most people experience inner healing as a gradual process that occurs over a period of time. Christ usually works with us as we become more open and responsive to his grace. In their book, *Healing Life's Hurts: Healing Memories Through the Five Stages of Forgiveness* (Paulist Press, 1978), Matthew and Dennis Linn point out that in Healing-of-Memories Prayer people generally go through the same five stages noted by Elisabeth Kübler-Ross. In her book, *On Death and Dying* (S&S Trade, 1993), she notes that people who are dying generally experience five stages of grief: denial, anger, bargaining, depression, and acceptance. As old and painful memories die, people experience these five stages. Even though it is possible for a memory to be healed all at once, in much the same way that some people seem to accept death immediately, most people go through the five stages over an indefinite time period.

In the case of painful memories, most people begin by denying the reality of the pain. In the second stage they generally blame others for hurting them. Next they set up conditions that need to be met before they will consider forgiveness or reconciliation. Fourth, they blame themselves for allowing the painful event or memory to cripple them. Finally they testify to the growth that occurred as a result of the healing of the memory.

People who have experienced serious losses or tremendous hurts in their lives sometimes experience these stages several times before healing finally occurs. Significant losses such as the death of a close family member, divorce, loss of job, loss of financial security, loss of health, or loss of youth are examples of some losses that take time to heal.

Many women today who are seeking healing after abortion, for example, discover that deep healing takes a lot of time and prayer. If you are seeking healing after an abortion, come before God, visualize your baby in the nurturing presence of God's motherly embrace. Release your baby to be forever loved beyond all comprehension by "Mother" God. You may need to repeat this prayer daily at first, then weekly, then monthly before experiencing healing.

One man moved back and forth through these stages several times over a period of five years before he was able to accept his divorce. His feelings of anger, resentment, guilt, hostility, and depression abated only after he regularly prayed for healing of memories. Gradually but ultimately, he came to experience peace and healing in his relationship with his former spouse.

The healing of a specific memory often happens over time and as a result of regular prayer. As you bring your hurtful memories before Christ, you are accepted as you are. Sharing your feelings at each stage of your journey— denial, anger, bargaining, depression, and acceptance— can provide you with new insights into Christ's healing love on your journey toward healing and wholeness.

❦ HEALING-OF-MEMORIES PRAYER

In this prayer form you will review a time in your life when you experienced a painful situation. If you experienced difficult relationships with your parents you may select a painful memory from childhood that needs healing. If you have issues that relate to your sexuality, you may find the source of this pain lies in memories of adolescent sexual experimentation. Perhaps you should focus on a recent rejection that seems to be crippling your effectiveness in your personal or professional life. You may need to pray about a painful argument with your spouse or a family member, an angry tirade with a coworker, a cutting remark from a close friend, or the loss of a friend or relative through death, sickness, or divorce.

If you use this prayer experience in a small group, be sure to allow sufficient time for all participants to get in touch with their thoughts and feelings. A series of dots (...) indicates a pause of several minutes during which participants can enter prayerful reflection.

PRAYER

Focus on one painful memory...Remember the memory in as much detail as you can...Be aware of the feelings you experience as this memory comes to life...Are you angry, jealous, anxious, depressed, hateful, fearful?... Share these feelings openly and honestly with Jesus...

Imagine that you are speaking to the other person or persons involved in your memory…Share your feelings with that person or those persons…

Invite God to come into the scene…Observe what God does…Listen…Allow yourself to say and do what you truly feel as the interaction takes place…Be receptive to the ways God is loving you in this memory…Be open to whatever God is saying or doing to heal you and the other person or persons involved in the hurtful event…

Conclude your prayer by thanking God for the healing you receive during this prayer time…

FURTHER REFLECTION

INDIVIDUAL

What feelings did I have as I prayed for healing?

What did God say or do to heal me? What did God say or do to heal the other person or persons involved in the memory? Did I experience reconciliation with the other person or persons?

What changes might I make as a result of this healing encounter with God?

How might I celebrate the healing that occurred during this prayer time?

GROUP

How do we react when we experience shame, blame, or guilt?

Why is it important to find healthy ways of dealing with shame and guilt?

How does this prayer experience bring us freedom and inner healing?

How can a painful event in life become a blessing?

How can Healing-of-Memories Prayer enable us to deal more effectively with anxiety, rejection, hurt, and failure?

FORGIVENESS PRAYER

To err is human, to forgive is divine. No matter how seriously we have sinned, God tenderly forgives us and constantly assures us of loving forgiveness.

> *Though your sins be like scarlet,*
> *they may become white as*
> *snow;*
> *Though they may be crimson*
> *red,*
> *they may become white as*
> *wool.*
>
> ISAIAH 1:18

Forgiving people was an integral part of the healing ministry of Jesus. Showing people how to give and receive forgiveness is an essential part of the proclamation of the gospel. If we do not experience the forgiving love of God for our sins and failures, we will not be able to forgive others. We cannot share with others what we ourselves do not have. We grow in the capacity to forgive others compassionately by experiencing the boundless, tender mercy of God for us in the moments in which we have failed and fallen short because of our weaknesses. While forgiveness is always difficult, the example of Christ on the Cross gives an example and a challenge to all Christians.

On the Cross, Christ demonstrates the nature of unconditional forgiveness when he promises heaven to the good thief. Christ does not demand an apology or set up a schedule for retribution. He simply says: "Amen, I say to you, today you will be with me in Paradise" (Luke 23:43). Likewise, Christ realizes that when we hurt others we are often unaware of the damage we inflict. He knew, for example, that those present at his crucifixion did not understand the horror of sin and evil or the meaning of salvation. His response to their ignorance is total forgiveness: "Father, forgive them, they know not what they do" (Luke 23:34).

When the rich young man decides to turn down his invitation to discipleship, Jesus does not give him a lecture on his lack of generosity or complain about the rejection he felt. Instead, Jesus looks at the man and loves him (Mark 10:17-22). Christ does not limit his love or forgiveness to those who do things his way. He loves people unconditionally, always accepting them as they are.

In the story of the prodigal son, the father does not become bitter with his son for leaving home, squandering his money, or embracing an irresponsible lifestyle. Rather, he patiently longs for his son's homecoming. When the son finally returns home, the father does not even wait for an apology or permit a confession. Embracing his son warmly, the forgiving father celebrates the beginning of a new and closer relationship with his son than he ever dreamed possible (Luke 15:11-32).

So often we find it difficult to forgive with the unconditional love of Christ because forgiveness seems to imply conditions. We use a variety of excuses: "I will forgive if she changes"; "I will forgive it he admits he was wrong and apologizes"; "I will forgive, but I will never forget the pain they have caused me." Such attitudes fall short of the ideal proposed in the Letter to the Ephesians: "Be kind to one another, compassionate, forgiving one another as God has forgiven you in Christ" (4:32). Christ, likewise, insists that we forgive every hurt (Matthew 18:21-22; Luke 6:27-42).

If we are to forgive others we cannot set conditions that they must meet. We must forget our desire for revenge and treat the person who has offended us with kindness and gentleness. In forgiving another person we begin by admitting that some perceived or real hurt has occurred. By offering forgiveness, however, we are saying that our relationship with the person who has offended us is of greater value to us than the pain we feel.

In the forgiveness process, it is also important to humbly admit that we, too, are sinners and that we have hurt and offended others. We should also keep in mind that it is only through the power of Jesus' death and resurrection that we can let go of our pain and allow his love to heal us.

An inability to forgive others for the hurts they have caused us leads to many psychological and physical diseases. These problems find their source, totally or in part, in bitterness, resentment, hostility, and unresolved conflict with others. These situations disturb our lives and often result in insomnia, headaches, stomach cramps, and neurotic and psychotic disorders. Forgiveness often is a key factor in freeing our body and mind to release the hostility that blocks spiritual growth.

A couple whose seventeen-year-old son was killed in an auto accident suffered much anguish and pain until they prayed for the grace to forgive. Their son fell asleep at the wheel after driving his friends home from a late night party. The couple were mired in grief and in the inability to forgive the other parents who had refused to pick up their children at the party. After several months of physical and mental anguish, the bereaved father said that he found the strength to forgive at the foot of the Cross of Christ. "I clung to Christ on the Cross, saw the tears in his eyes, and knew that he shared my loss. At that moment I forgave, and a burden was lifted from my heart."

A young woman was greatly distressed after learning that she was pregnant and that her husband was diagnosed as having AIDS. She was angry at her husband and feared that she and the baby might be infected. In her desperation she considered an abortion. After several weeks of prayer and counseling, the woman shared one of her prayer experiences: "I told Jesus that my heart was broken like his on the Cross, and I could no longer bear the pain. Yet, somehow I sensed that he was really with me and loved me." After this the woman was able to forgive her husband, support him in his struggle with this serious disease, and plan for their baby's birth.

Understanding Forgiveness Prayer

Approaching Jesus' Cross with your difficulties is one powerful way to pray for forgiveness. While this is not the only approach to forgiveness, it is a good place to start. You know that Jesus forgave your sins when he died on the Cross, but remember, too, that it is from the same Cross that Jesus forgives those who hurt you.

In this prayer you imagine yourself on Calvary, walking up to the Cross and kneeling at the feet of Jesus. Through your imagination you look at Jesus' wounds and experience the suffering he endured for you, since before you forgive others you need to accept Jesus' loving forgiveness in your own life.

After accepting Christ's forgiveness you can share with others that which you have received yourself. Imagine the person with whom you need reconciliation approaching Jesus on the Cross. Allow yourself to become involved intellectually, emotionally, and spiritually in this scene. Realize that this moment of forgiveness is a gift from Jesus that you cannot produce by your own efforts.

Since each of us has been damaged by our own sins and the sins committed against us, we are unable to forgive others by our own power. Seeking God's forgiveness is an experience of empowerment unsurpassed in the Christian life. We need the forgiveness that flowed through Jesus on the Cross. Forgiveness Prayer helps us let go of hurt feelings, understand how the perspectives of others may be different from ours, and reconcile people to a place of love in our hearts. Forgiveness Prayer is one way we can come before the Cross of Christ to ask him to give us this gift of forgiveness and reconciliation.

 FORGIVENESS PRAYER

In this prayer approach to inner healing you can pray about a painful relationship in which you are dealing with anger or resentment.

If you use this prayer experience in a small group, be sure to allow sufficient time for all participants to get in touch with their thoughts and feelings. A series of dots (…) indicates a pause of several minutes during which participants can enter prayerful reflection.

PRAYER

Imagine that the person you are angry with is standing or sitting in front of you…

Share with this person all the hostility you feel…

After you have shared all your anger and resentment with the other person, look at the situation from the other person's viewpoint. Try to get into his or her pain and explain the incident or relationship from his or her perspective…How did the other person feel?…Why did he or she hurt you?…

See Jesus on the Cross…Visualize the physical agony…the nails in his feet and hands…the crown of thorns pressed in at his temples…Listen to the sounds… Jesus' labored and pained breathing…the soldiers talking and laughing…the words of Mary and the Beloved Disciple…the sobs of those who love Jesus…Look at the faithful women who are present…Mary of Magdala… Mary, Jesus' mother…Mary, the wife of Clopas…

Be aware of how you feel as you experience the pain of Jesus' sufferings on the Cross…What do you want to say to him?…How do you want to comfort him?…What attitudes or relationships in your life need his forgiveness?…

Spend as much time as you wish at the foot of the Cross conversing with the Crucified Savior…

Recall your own anger and resentment, and share that with Jesus…Ask Jesus to show you where you are hurt and how you are reacting to that hurt…Express your anger and resentment in whatever way seems most appropriate. (Do not be afraid to use emotional language. You can even yell, scream, cry, or shout. The important thing is to express openly your feelings to Jesus. Don't worry; Jesus can handle your pain. He will not be shocked at anything you share.)

Spend as long a time as you wish sharing your anger and resentment with Jesus…Listen to his loving response to you…Invite Jesus to embrace you in your hurt and pain…

Imagine the person with whom you are angry walking up the hill of Calvary toward you…How do you feel as you see this person approach Jesus on the Cross?…What does Jesus say or do to that person?…Allow the forgiveness of Jesus on the Cross to touch you in whatever way seems most real…Ask Jesus to help you see the other person and yourself with loving compassion…

Listen as Jesus speaks healing words of forgiveness to both of you: "Father, forgive him, he did not know what he was doing"…"Father, forgive her, she did not know what she was doing"…"Father, forgive them, they did not know what they were doing." Allow yourself to enter fully into this prayer of Jesus until you can pray it with Jesus for the other person…Ask Jesus to fill your heart with tender mercy and divine compassion toward this person…

Look into the eyes of Jesus, and share with him the thoughts and feelings of your heart…Look into the eyes of your brother or sister with whom you are angry, and share your thoughts and feelings…

 **FURTHER REFLECTION**

INDIVIDUAL

What feelings did I have as I participated in this prayer of forgiveness?

What did Jesus say or do to heal me?

How did I experience the person with whom I was angry?

Will there be any changes in our relationship as a result of this prayer experience?

How can I celebrate the forgiveness I have experienced in this prayer? (Consider writing a letter to the person who hurt you or inviting the person to a special meal or performing a secret act of kindness for the person.)

GROUP

How does Forgiveness Prayer reveal new insights into Jesus' love for us?

How can we help others experience God's tender mercies in their lives?

How can we be signs of God's forgiveness to the world?

How can Forgiveness Prayer be effective in healing resentment and anger in relationships?

Where have we witnessed examples of spiritual growth that resulted from forgiveness in our own lives or in the lives of our families or friends?

(If you experience a return of anger or resentment in the days or weeks after you pray this prayer, repeat this or another healing prayer form. It takes time for deep wounds to be healed, and generally more than one prayer experience is necessary for complete healing to occur. If after several attempts with this prayer form your anger and resentment continue to cause problems, seek out a competent counselor or spiritual director.)

JOURNAL PRAYER

A journal is a record of significant insights, reflections, prayers, dreams, and religious experiences—all products of our inner lives. A journal reflects the movements of our minds and spirits, the stirrings of the Spirit within us, and the result of God's grace in the events of our lives. When we write a journal we ask ourselves "What are the important thoughts and feelings that I have about this relationship or occurrence?"

Keeping a journal helps us become more conscious of the spiritual meaning of particular events in our lives. Somewhere in the midst of our hectic daily routines it is good to take time to reflect on the deeper significance of certain occurrences so we can put them into perspective and comprehend their value in the light of eternity. Writing our emotions, feelings, sensations, and thoughts can help us become more sensitive to ourselves, other persons, and God.

Through journal keeping we can also discover what really occurred in an experience because we remember in a different way, recalling all that our senses experienced. This takes time and results in a deepening appreciation for the treasured gift of every moment of life. A journal is a tool that helps us toward this end. Using both the senses and imagination we look at the event from the inside and not as a bystander. As we write about these experiences they become clearer and more meaningful—more so than our mere thought processes can net.

Journal Prayer helped a young woman who was extremely angry and upset at being rejected by her boyfriend. She was physically attractive, intelligent, and had a promising career. Since she was approaching her late thirties, she worried that she would never be married. For several years she had put all her energies into developing close relationships with male friends, hoping to find the right person with whom she could enjoy total happiness and fulfillment. Instead, she experienced several heartbreaking entanglements that caused her bitter disappointment.

After trying several different healing prayer forms, Journal Prayer helped this woman discover her own self-worth and find ways in which she could live a more fulfilling life. Journal Prayer helped her discover Jesus' presence in her lonely moments and made it clear to her that no one else could totally fulfill her. Her journal became a tool in which she was able to encounter her fear of rejection and look at some of the dark corners in her own heart. This led her to invite Jesus into these painful areas to free and heal her. As a result of her journal, the woman grew less possessive and fearful of rejection. She also came to a greater appreciation of the power of intimacy and the value of close relationships in her life.

As Christians we gain insights from our own intuitive powers, as well as from the presence of Christ living within us and constantly speaking to us from the depths of our being. In this prayer style we can invite Jesus to use our intuition and creative powers to reveal areas of our lives that need his healing touch. Some examples of areas that might need deeper healing through Journal Prayer are: distorted images of our masculinity or femininity, painful sexual encounters or relationships, compulsive behavioral patterns, problems with intimacy, or inability to express feelings.

Journaling about problem areas in our lives that need healing can help us grow for two reasons. First, journaling helps us reflect on and become aware of the meaning of our experiences and behavior patterns. When we have an experience and then express it in some tangible way, the experience becomes more deeply our own. If the incident involves guilt or feelings of inadequacy or powerlessness, it is important to bring these wounded areas of our life to Christ, to share our feelings in some concrete way with our Savior, and to open ourselves to divine healing. Second, journaling in an atmosphere of prayer can utilize the intuitive powers of the mind. These powers can be sources of spiritual experiences that reveal to us our inner selves.

Understanding Journal Prayer

There are a number of different ways to keep a journal. One writer suggests that beginners make a graph of their religious experiences by creating a time line. At the far left side of an oblong sheet of paper write "Birth" and at the far right side write "Today." As you move from "Birth" to "Today," identify times in your life when you experienced deep faith in God's presence, as well as those moments when you felt sadness and experienced diffi-culty. Reflect on events that have had an impact on your family relationships, your educational pursuits, your work experiences, your choice of vocation, your spirituality, and so forth. Concentrate on the high and the low times that stand out in your life journey, the purpose being to help you honestly focus on your own religious experiences.

There are several other ways to keep a prayer journal. You can write a letter to God, sharing some of your intimate thoughts. You might share your daily activities, feelings, joys, and sorrows, or you might simply explain to the Holy One how certain significant relationships are influencing your life.

Because dreams reveal truths about our attitudes and feelings that intellectual analysis can rarely accomplish, you may want to use your dreams as a source of material for journaling. Write the content of your dreams, and ask Jesus to assist you in dream interpretation: the meaning or symbolic significance of characters, events, and locations. In your journal, record this dialogue between you and God. Recording the insights revealed in your encounter with God can help you become a more integrated person.

Regardless of the journal style you select, honesty is critical. Look into the depths of your heart to see both your strengths and your weaknesses; acknowledge their presence, and accept responsibility for them. Rather than making you feel insecure, this exercise will put you in touch with God's affirming presence. Do not write to impress others, but to see yourself as you really are: a unique and beautiful reflection of the divine image.

JOURNAL PRAYER

If you use this prayer experience in a small group, be sure to allow sufficient time for all participants to get in touch with their thoughts and feelings. A series of dots (…) indicates a pause of several minutes during which participants can enter prayerful reflection.

PRAYER

Allow your body to relax…Feel your head and neck relax…Relax your eyes, mouth, and chin…Let go of tension in the back of your neck and your shoulders… Feel your arms and hands relax…Relax your back and chest…

Feel relaxation pouring through your stomach, hips, and knees…Feel your legs, ankles, feet, and toes becoming relaxed…

(Repeat this exercise if you notice that any tense areas remain.)

Write a letter to God about an area of your life in which you need healing. Look at the times when you were most appreciative of God's help in your life, times you felt loved and empowered by God. Look at those times when you struggled with doubt, temptation, confusion, anger, loneliness. Share your feelings with God. Be open and honest.

(Do not be concerned about writing complete sentences, and do not worry about spelling, punctuation, or how correctly you write. Write freely and honestly without judgment, trusting God's compassionate healing love to touch your spirit. What you write in your journal is confidential unless you personally choose to let others read what you have written. No one will ask you to share the contents. Even in a small group you will not be asked to share the contents of your journal. You will share only how journaling as a prayer style "fits" your spiritual needs.)

Allow God to communicate with you in a return letter. (You might actually write this letter or simply hear it in your heart.)

(Many often wonder if God is really responding in this prayer or if it's their imagination. It is the belief of many wise healing ministers that any words that help you know you are loved and that lead you to greater holiness come from the love and wisdom of God. These teachers explain that Journal Prayer can be as simple as writing a love letter to God, and listening to the love letter God writes to you.)

 FURTHER REFLECTION

INDIVIDUAL

How did I feel as I wrote my letter to God sharing my need for healing?

How did I feel as I read (heard) God's response?

Have I become more aware of God's Spirit dwelling within me?

Have I experienced God as my healer who embraces me with tender love?

GROUP

How can Journal Prayer help us become more aware that God dwells within us and loves us?

What obstacles get in the way of experiencing God's healing love in our lives?

How can Journal Prayer help us "hear" God's voice?

In what areas of life could Journal Prayer help us deal more effectively with hurts and problems and find healing?

How can Journal Prayer help us reflect on the spiritual meaning of our dreams? How can this be an effective tool for spiritual growth?

CENTERING PRAYER

Centering Prayer can be characterized as a passive, relaxing form of prayer. Rather than concentrating our imagination, thoughts, and feelings on certain passages from Scripture or on selected spiritual readings in order to gain insights into God, Centering Prayer focuses on waiting upon God in silence, and contemplating the divine presence. This form of contemplative prayer takes us beyond thoughts, words, and images into the very embrace of God. In Centering Prayer we let go of our own feelings and thoughts and unite our hearts and wills with God. We allow Christ's Spirit to come alive in us. "As proof that you are children, God sent the spirit of [the First Born] into our hearts, crying out, 'Abba, [God]!' " (Galatians 4:6). Christ's Spirit becomes our spirit in such a way that Christ becomes more intimately present to us than we are to ourselves. "I live, no longer I, but Christ lives in me" (Galatians 2:20).

Centering Prayer offers an experience of God's love for us and our own lovableness in the eyes of God. It can free us from tension and stress, help us trust in God's love, and lead us toward healing and wholeness. Because it is a simple, childlike prayer that opens us to the treasures of the heavenly kingdom, Centering Prayer allows us to rejoice in God's loving embrace. Jesus stressed the importance of this in the gospel when he said, "Let the children come to me and do not prevent them; for the [Reign] of God belongs to such as these" (Luke 18:16).

Centering Prayer provides a method that allows us to let go of distractions and to focus on the Beloved. In this prayer experience we strive to enter into a state of gentle awareness of God's loving presence dwelling within the center of our being.

Centering Prayer is a modern term that describes an ancient form of prayer referred to in a medieval mystical classic, *The Cloud of Unknowing.* The unknown author of *The Cloud of Unknowing* describes the path to contemplation in these words:

> *Lift up your heart to the Lord, with a gentle stirring of love desiring him for his own sake and not for his gifts. Center all your attention and desire on him and let this be the sole concern of your mind and heart. Do all in your power to forget everything else, keeping your thoughts and desires free from involvement with any of God's creatures or their affairs whether in general or in particular.*

CHAPTER 3

In his recent book, *Centering Prayer: Renewing an Ancient Christian Prayer Form* (Doubleday, 1982), M. Basil Pennington provides a three-rule formula for Centering Prayer. Rule one requires that we become quiet and aware of God's presence dwelling within us. He suggests that we begin the prayer by saying something like, "Thank you

God, for your presence in the depths of my being."
Pennington reminds pray-ers to keep the prayer simple and
to let it come from the heart, remembering that God is the
initiator inviting us into a deeper love relationship.

Rule two provides help with distractions. Since
distracting thoughts and images may come to disrupt our
quiet attentiveness to God, this rule suggests use of a
prayer word to refocus our being on the love and presence
of God. When distractions come, when we drift from
God, when we no longer feel God's loving embrace, we
simply use a single word or sound to experience again the
loving presence of God. This return to the center of our
being can come through using a word, a sigh, or an
unintelligible sound. Some popular prayer words are:
"Jesus," "Father," "Mother," "God," or "love." The prayer
word can be changed at any time. Pray-ers might use one
word on one day and a different word on some other day.

Rule three instructs us to repeat the prayer word
gently when we become aware of being distracted. When
we become aware of anything—thoughts, feelings,
images—we simply let go of them by gently reciting the
prayer word. There may be times during Centering Prayer
when a prayer word isn't used; at other times, we may
wish to recite it often. We should not be discouraged if
many distractions occur during Centering Prayer; this is
normal. The frequency with which we recite the prayer
word is not important. Rather, remaining focused on God
dwelling within is the main purpose, and the prayer word
is a means of maintaining that focus. Pray-ers do well,
too, to remember that the effectiveness of prayer is not
measured by the absence of distractions, but in the
growth of love for God and neighbor in everyday life.

Before trying this prayer style it is necessary to relax
and find a quiet place, free of excessive noise and distractions. Even though we can use Centering Prayer in a busy
airport or train station, it is best to select a quiet, calm

place. Some people like to pray in the privacy of their bedroom, den, bathroom, or basement. Other people choose their office or an empty room in the building where they are employed. One young mother prays in her kitchen after the children have gone to school. A busy executive likes to use Centering Prayer during his flights from city to city. As the plane glides through the clouds, he closes his eyes, repeats his prayer word, and rests in God's embrace. Different places work for different people. We must find the place that is right for us and that provides a suitable environment for quiet prayer.

Time is also a significant factor in Centering Prayer. Some people like to use Centering Prayer during the early morning hours; others choose to pray instead of taking a coffee or lunch break. Some select the early evening hours before dinner, and still others like the late night hours. One woman gets up in the middle of the night for twenty minutes of Centering Prayer. She likes the quiet of those hours and claims that she wakes up more refreshed in the morning than if she had not interrupted her sleep to pray. The only time that is not recommended for this prayer form is after a meal when the body is engaged in the process of digestion. Some people who have tried this prayer after a heavy meal complain that they end up taking a nice nap.

Posture, too, is important. A chair that supports the back and keeps it straight is best. Most people feel comfortable and relaxed in this position. Some people select positions recommended by Eastern mystics or taught in contemporary yoga or Zen meditation groups. Others like to lie flat on their bed or on a mat on the floor. The posture must simply be conducive to prayer.

Understanding Centering Prayer

Centering Prayer brings a great sense of peace to many people. They testify to a lessening of stress and tension and to a greater tranquillity and peace in their lives. One man who was undergoing psychotherapy found a marked improvement in treatment after he started to use Centering Prayer. "It was like discovering a still point within the turmoil of my life that calmed all my fears."

Physical and emotional well-being is a another benefit that can come from using Centering Prayer. When a group of men and women who worked in high stress-related jobs learned how to use Centering Prayer, they discovered a lowering of blood pressure, a more positive outlook, and a reduction of anxiety after a short time of using this prayer form.

Centering Prayer helps people develop a greater awareness of God's indwelling presence within the depths of their hearts. Many men and women claim that Centering Prayer has given them a deeper appreciation of God's special closeness to them.

Centering Prayer can also bring clear and direct inner healing into people's lives. One woman who used to scream at her children for small offenses said that Centering Prayer helped her become calm and more patient with the minor disturbances of family life. An older priest said that this prayer helped him be gentler with parishioners who constantly complained and got on his nerves. A husband said that after he started to use Centering Prayer regularly he became less critical and more loving toward his wife. A young professional woman observed that Centering Prayer aided her in becoming less fearful and more confident in making decisions that would affect the lives of her subordinates. A seminary spiritual director observed that Centering Prayer helped him become less judgmental and more compassionate in his ministry with young men interested in the priesthood.

The most important effects of Centering Prayer, however, are growth in love of God and others. God will always take the initiative in inviting you into deeper intimacy. Centering Prayer is one way you can respond to this call. As you give yourself wholeheartedly to God present within, you discover that the relationships and events of life are gradually transformed. You become a more loving and vibrant witness to the gospel.

CENTERING PRAYER

If you use this prayer experience in a small group, be sure to allow sufficient time for all participants to get in touch with their thoughts and feelings. A series of dots (…) indicates a pause of several minutes during which participants can enter prayerful reflection.

PRAYER

Be attentive to your breathing…Breathe in…Breathe out…As you breathe in, breathe in the boundless love of God…As you breathe out, breathe out anger, resentment, anxiety…Breathe in God's infinite, passionate love for you…Breathe out fear, anger, resentment…

(Repeat this exercise until you feel relaxed and ready to start your Centering Prayer.)

Recall the presence of God dwelling in the depths of your being. Make up a simple prayer from your heart that reminds you of God's nearness. For example, "O God, I know that you are present within me always loving me. Help me to delight in your love for me and to give myself totally to you this day."

After becoming aware of God's presence dwelling within you, quietly and slowly repeat to yourself a simple, single prayer word that expresses your response to God's love. (The purpose of this prayer word is to help you empty your mind and heart so that God can fill you with healing love. The prayer word assists you in finding inner silence. It should be a simple word like "love," "God," or "Jesus." It should not be a word that causes distracting images or thoughts.)

Simply *be* in love with God. (When you become aware of anything else during the time of your prayer, simply and gently return to your prayer word. View Centering Prayer as a prayer of the heart. Imagine yourself sitting quietly in the presence of a friend whom you dearly cherish. No words are necessary. It's enough to be together, enjoying each other's company in deep love.)

Conclude the experience of Centering Prayer by taking several minutes to slowly pray the Lord's Prayer or some other prayer. Then notice the healing and peace that has come to dwell in the center of your being.

 FURTHER REFLECTION

INDIVIDUAL

Did Centering Prayer help me experience God's indwelling presence in a new way?

Was my prayer word helpful in keeping me centered and in dealing with distractions?

Does contemplative prayer appeal to me? Why or why not?

How can Centering Prayer help me become more peaceful?

GROUP

How can Centering Prayer help us experience inner healing in the midst of the pressures of contemporary life?

As we look at our world today, where is the need for healing especially evident?

How can Centering Prayer help us become more aware of God's indwelling presence?

How can Centering Prayer have a healing effect upon our minds and bodies?

SCRIPTURE PRAYER

We often read Scripture from an outsider's perspective, remaining at a distance from its teachings and stories, yet trying to comprehend its meaning for our lives. This external approach goes against the Gospel of John, which tells us to make God's Word our dwelling place: "If you remain in my word, you will truly be my disciples" (8:31). This implies that we are to become participants and not remain mere observers.

Entering into the Word of God takes imagination. Through imaginative prayer we walk inside the gospel passage to become one with those who are involved in the scene. Praying Scripture with the imagination means entering into the details and emotions of the passage and listening as God speaks from within the text. This form of prayer can help us experience the Word of God as living and vibrant in our lives. As we pray Scripture using the gift of our imagination, we can see ourselves in the various characters in the story.

Deep within each of us there is a hunger for an intimate, personal relationship with God. Through Scripture we can begin to recognize God's loving presence everywhere. A real transformation can occur as our personal relationship with God grows, and we develop a fresh spiritual way of thinking. We adopt the mind and heart of Christ.

As we pray the Scriptures, we encounter a God who is revealed as a compassionate, loving, healing Lord. We learn that we are totally and unconditionally accepted, just as we are, with our own unique gifts and weaknesses. In the Scriptures we hear God's Word offering a message of love and hope for each of us personally. In this prayer form our attitude should be: "What is God's message for me now?" As we listen to God's Word we are strengthened and challenged to live a life of holiness, healed of past hurts and sinfulness. "All scripture is inspired by God and is useful for teaching, for refutation, for correction, and for training in righteousness, so that one who belongs to God may be competent, equipped for every good work" (2 Timothy 3:16-17).

Jesus emphasizes the importance of listening to the Word of God in our lives. On one occasion, as he was teaching, a woman called out: "Blessed is the womb that carried you and the breasts at which you nursed" (Luke 11:27). Jesus responded: "Rather, blessed are those who hear the word of God and observe it" (Luke 11:28). According to Jesus, what really matters is knowing the Word of God and putting it into practice.

Understanding Scripture Prayer

How do you go about listening to the Word of God and using it to find healing from past hurts and sinful ways? Start by obtaining a good Bible with a sound translation that reflects recent studies in the areas of archaeology, history, and literary criticism. Most bookstores carry a variety of Bibles that provide this kind of credibility.

To help you determine which passages of Scripture to pray with, simply select a few favorites, focus on the liturgical readings for the coming Sunday, or use a monthly Scripture guide such as *Share the Word* (3031 Fourth Street, N.E.; Washington, DC 20017) or *Praying* (National Catholic Reporter, Kansas City, Missouri). Some people find it helpful to consult with their pastor, teacher, spiritual director, or religious educator in choosing passages from the Bible that will be meaningful for their life situations.

Once you have selected a passage that will be beneficial to your spiritual growth, choose a quiet place and a comfortable posture. When you create space through quieting yourself, Scripture begins to speak to you in a powerful way. In such an atmosphere you can bathe yourself in the Word and experience the healing power of God's love touching your life. One woman describes this need for healing in a letter she wrote:

> *For the last three years I have been angry and bitter toward my husband for his alcoholism which has destroyed our home. Most days I hated waking up as I never knew how bad he was going to be. Our home was filled with fighting, constant arguments, and turmoil. Things improved after I started to concentrate on my own recovery in the Al-Anon program, but I still feel lonely and empty inside and in need of deep healing.*

It was suggested to this woman that she select a gospel passage that described a time when Jesus faced loneliness in his life. A month later the woman shared how she had spent some prayer time meditating on Jesus in the Garden of Gethsemane. As she entered into Jesus' agony with him, she tried to console him. In that space of pain and compassion, the woman discovered a new appreciation of the intense suffering Jesus endured. Later she shared:

"The more I felt his loneliness within my heart, the more I knew how deeply he loved me and how much he wanted to comfort and heal me."

Entering the scene as an eyewitness, as this woman did, and watching the story happen as if you were there is one approach to Scripture Prayer. This involves reading each section of the story in a way in which you become part of it. An alternate approach would be to take the place of the person to whom Jesus speaks or touches with his healing love. In this way you can open yourself to receive the same healing love that Jesus showed to the person in the Scriptures. You might want to take on the role of Jesus in the scene. Since Jesus tells us, "You are in me and I in you" (John 14:20), you know that his sufferings bring healing to your hurt; your depression is healed in his agony; your rejection is healed in the rejection he felt during his public life.

After you decide how you are going to participate in the Scripture story, read the verses quietly and reflectively, using the gifts of your imagination. Listen to the words that are spoken, and notice the tone of voice. See the faces of the people involved in the scene, and observe body movements and gestures that reveal feelings and attitudes. Ask the Holy Spirit for guidance as you experience the activity of the story and the sights, sounds, smells, and feelings, as if they were your own experiences.

When you use Scripture Prayer you pray that the gospel event will have the same healing and strengthening effect on you as it did in the Scriptures. Jesus' story becomes your story. His healing love touches you in the same way it touched the people he encountered on his earthly journey. Like people in the gospels, your openness to the healing power of Jesus can loosen the grip of resentment, anxiety, and depression, allowing kindness, hope, and joy to heal your wounds.

A middle-aged, single woman, successful with her business career, had an experience of Scripture Prayer that changed her life. For years she has been filled with jealousy toward her younger married sister, a housewife with three children. Growing up, they had competed for their parents' affections and had fought over make-up, boyfriends, and school activities. They were sisters, but they were very different people who saw life from opposite perspectives.

As the woman prayerfully reflected on the Mary and Martha story (Luke 10:38-42), she realized that she had always envied her sister's carefree, loving personality. As she entered this gospel scene, she identified with Martha and saw her sister as Mary. She experienced the anxieties of Martha and felt the compassion of Christ touch her as she listened to his words: "Martha, Martha, you are anxious and worried about many things. There is need of only one thing" (Luke 10:41-42). Entering into the scene and watching Jesus accept and love Martha—the worrier—the woman felt accepted and loved as well. She felt that Jesus understood that she, like Martha, had burdens of anxiety that were difficult to surrender. She listened as Christ praised her for using her gifts as a good steward and expressed his desire to heal her from her needless anxiety and jealousy.

As the woman continued to pray, she took on the identity of Mary. Sitting before the Lord she felt a new sense of peace and relaxation envelop her entire being. Jesus' words to Mary took on new meaning: "Mary has chosen the better part and it will not be taken from her" (Luke 10:42). The woman realized that she did not have to compete with her sister or anyone else to be happy. She could affirm her own giftedness and, at the same time, recognize the giftedness of her sister. Gradually, this woman was able to begin a new relationship with her sister.

There are other ways to use Scripture Prayer. You might try meditating on the poetic verses of the psalms, or select a brief Scripture passage that has special meaning for your life. If you are worried about past sins or weaknesses, consider choosing a Scripture passage that assures you of God's loving mercy, such as: "Though your sins be like scarlet, they may become white as snow" (Isaiah 1:18).

Another form of Scripture Prayer involves groups of people praying with the Scriptures. The group meets to read the Scripture passages of the following Sunday's liturgy. The reading is followed by a presentation of the Scripture's background and a group discussion. Then the group prayerfully reflects on the meaning of God's Word in their lives. This process can have a powerful healing and peace-giving effect as members of a Christian community assist one another in hearing and understanding God's Word.

If you find it difficult to quietly listen to and understand the voice of God in Scripture, do not be discouraged; you are in excellent company! Even though the apostles walked and talked with Jesus, they often missed his message. When Jesus told the Twelve that he would have to suffer much and be put to death, they didn't understand. They found it difficult to judge situations by God's standards. "At this he turned around and, looking at his disciples, rebuked Peter and said, 'Get behind me, Satan. You are thinking not as God does, but as human beings do'" (Mark 8:33). Thinking like Jesus doesn't happen overnight, but comes with the regular use of Scripture Prayer.

These well-known passages may help you begin using Scripture Prayer. The individual verse can be used alone, or the entire passage surrounding the verse can serve as a scene to contemplate.

You, [God], are near to all who call upon you....
　　You hear their cry and save them.

PSALM 145:18,19

I have called you by name: you are mine....
　　You are precious in my eyes...
　　I love you.

ISAIAH 43:1,4

[God] called me from birth....
　　I will never forget you.

ISAIAH 49:1,15

Before I formed you in the womb I knew you.

JEREMIAH 1:5

I will be their God, and they shall be my people.

JEREMIAH 31:33

I myself will look after and tend my sheep.

EZEKIEL 34:11

I will lead her into the desert
and speak to her heart.

HOSEA 2:16

I fostered them like one
　　who raises an infant to his cheeks.

HOSEA 11:4

So I tell you, her many sins have been forgiven; hence, she has shown great love. But the one to whom little is forgiven, loves little.

LUKE 7:47

Stay with us, for it is nearly evening.

LUKE 24:29

For wisdom is more mobile than any motion;
because of her pureness she pervades and penetrates all
       things.
For she is a breath of the power of God.

WISDOM 7:24-25 (NRSV)

[I pray] that they may all be one, as you, [Abba, God], are
in me and I in you.

JOHN 17:21

Do you love me?

JOHN 21:17

And they were all filled with the holy Spirit.

ACTS OF THE APOSTLES 2:4

We know that all things work for good for those who love
God, who are called according to [God's] purpose.

ROMANS 8:28

Who will separate us from the love of Christ? Will
[trouble], or distress, or persecution, or [hunger], or
nakedness, or [danger], or [violence]?

ROMANS 8:35 (NRSV)

For I am convinced that neither death nor life, nor
angels...nor things present, nor things to come...nor
anything else in all creation, will be able to separate us
from the love of God in Christ Jesus...

ROMANS 8:38,39 (NRSV)

Perfect love drives out fear.

1 JOHN 4:18

 SCRIPTURE PRAYER

Choose a Scripture passage that will meet your needs. The story of the penitent woman (Luke 7:36-50) will be used to illustrate this approach to Scripture Prayer. Read the passage slowly, as you would read a personal letter from a friend who loves you deeply. You may want to read the passage more than once. (If Scripture Prayer is done in a group, one person should read the passage aloud.)

Enter whatever part of the scene in the passage touches you most deeply. You can choose to become the woman, Simon the Pharisee, Jesus, a dinner guest, or you can enter the story as yourself. Simply keep in mind that there is no "correct way" of praying by using your imagination. The following steps provide only a guide, a help to encounter Jesus in the Scriptures. There are no "right images" or ways that you must behave in this style of prayer. Come before the Healer as you are, and allow Christ to interact with you or the character you choose to identify with in the story.

If you use this prayer experience in a small group, be sure to allow sufficient time for all participants to get in touch with their thoughts and feelings. A series of dots (...) indicates a pause of several minutes during which participants can enter prayerful reflection.

PRAYER

Use your senses and imagination to experience the scene fully. Smell the aroma of the food...the perfumed oil... Look at the faces of the people at the dinner table... Simon the host...Jesus...the woman...

Listen to the sounds of the guests talking...the laughter... the music...

Feel the compassionate touch of Jesus…the coldness of Simon's greeting…the warmth of the woman's love…

Focus more closely on the identity of one person (the penitent woman, Jesus, Simon, another guest)…Be aware of how you feel as you relive this scene…As the woman, how does it feel to walk into the room with your vase of perfumed oil…weeping…kissing Jesus' feet…perfuming his feet with the oil…listening to Simon's criticism… listening to Jesus' reply to Simon…looking into Jesus' eyes…experiencing boundless mercy?…

As Jesus, how do you feel when the woman enters the room…stands behind you…weeps…kisses your feet…perfumes your feet with oil?…Do you feel disappointment with Simon's behavior?…How do you feel about the other dinner guests?…How do you feel as you tell the woman: "Your sins are forgiven…Your faith has saved you; go in peace"?…

As Simon, how do you feel when Jesus arrives in your home?…How do you feel when the woman comes unannounced to the dinner?…How do you feel as she weeps…kisses Jesus' feet?…How do you feel as Jesus shares his disappointment over your inhospitable behavior?…What do you learn about God's forgiveness from Jesus?…If you were to schedule another dinner party and invite Jesus to be present, would you do anything differently?…

As yourself, what do you say or do to Jesus?…What does he say or do to you?…Which areas of your life need his forgiveness?…What does he say or do that heals you?…How does he minister to your needs?…What does Jesus want of you in this moment?…

Conclude your prayer time by giving thanks for whatever Christ did for you...

(Even if your prayer was filled with distractions and you had a difficult time "getting into the scene," remember that your prayer and spiritual growth depend primarily on God's grace. Your role is simply to be receptive and open to whatever healing God may wish to accomplish within you. Ask Jesus to create within your heart a deeper hunger for the healing gift of the Word of God.)

 FURTHER REFLECTION

INDIVIDUAL

What is God revealing to me about God's forgiving love in this story?

Did I experience healing in this encounter with Christ?

What are the areas in my life where I need forgiveness and healing? where growth is impeded by past hurts and blockages of God's grace?

What feelings arise in me when I reflect on God's boundless mercy in my life?

GROUP

How can Scripture Prayer help us experience God's love in a new or exciting way?

What is it like to enter a Scripture scene with our senses?

What difficulties arose? Are we able to exercise some senses easier than others?

What are the advantages of taking on different identities in this kind of prayer?

How can this type of prayer make the Scriptures more vivid and meaningful?

How can Scripture Prayer have a healing effect on us? on others?

FANTASY PRAYER

Fantasy Prayer utilizes our hyperactive memory and anxious imagination to enhance experiences of prayer. Instead of being a source of distraction filling us with apprehension over the future or the past, imagination can assist us to focus on the possibilities that can occur within the situation. We can use the gifts of memory and imagination to create an atmosphere of expectation and faith in God's power. With this prayer form we can see the powerful healing presence of God in all the events of our lives— past, present, and future.

The images we have of ourselves prepare us for success or for failure; we live our lives based on our self-images. Very often these perceptions come from parents, teachers, or people who have influenced our early years. Some familiar negative thought patterns that can block us from loving ourselves, others, and God are: "I'm not intelligent enough"; "I'm not attractive enough"; "If you really knew me you wouldn't love me"; "It's too risky...I might fail"; "What will the neighbors say?" When we listen to these negative thoughts we risk accepting them as facts, which in turn impedes our growth and wholeness.

Fantasy Prayer is an effective way of using our imaginations to help us break free of these negative thoughts, and to visualize the power of God's healing love replacing them with positive, creative thoughts. When Christ said, "I am with you always" (Matthew 28:20), he promised that he would be with us as we cleanse our minds of these negative thoughts and open ourselves to his healing power. Aware of Jesus' desire to heal us, we can use Fantasy Prayer to help us reflect on some new life-giving affirmations about ourselves: "I can break free of old, negative feelings"; "I am loved totally by God"; "I forgive myself and others"; "I prefer to feel peace and love instead of anger and resentment"; "I am a lovable and loving person."

In his book *Power of Your Subconscious Mind* (Prentice Hall, 1988), Dr. Joseph Murphy, shares this beautiful and healing affirmation:

> My body and all its organs were created by a Higher Power. It knows how to heal me. Its wisdom fashioned all my organs, tissues, muscles, and bones. The infinite healing presence within me is now transforming every atom of my being, making me whole and perfect now.
>
> I give thanks for the healing I know is taking place now. Wonderful are the works of a Power greater than myself, the God…within me.

Fantasy Prayer provides a context for a peaceful, hopeful, healing encounter with God. As a prayer style, Fantasy Prayer sets the stage for deeper levels of prayer. It prepares us for whatever way God may wish to bring healing. In Fantasy Prayer there is no "right" or "wrong" way to pray. The options are limitless. One approach to

Fantasy Prayer involves picturing a scene, such as a peaceful meadow, a quiet lake, a picturesque mountain, or a lovely beach, then imaging Jesus entering the scene. In the scene, we listen to what Jesus says and note how we feel.

Understanding Fantasy Prayer

Suppose you are frightened and want to experience the healing love of Christ. You could create an imaginary story of an encounter with Jesus on a grassy hillside. See the plush, green carpet mountain and the fluffy white clouds. Feel the cool breeze and warm sun. Hear the chirping of the birds. Smell the scent of wildflowers. Then imagine Jesus climbing the hill with you, listening to you as you share your anxieties, and healing each anxiety in his care.

In another form of Fantasy Prayer, you might use Christian religious settings or images that reflect deep longings, hopes, and dreams for an encounter with God. When using religious images in Fantasy Prayer several things become clear. First, religious imagery reveals God and helps you become conscious of both the immanent and transcendent qualities of God. The Lord who is an intimate friend and lover is, at the same time, the glorious, majestic Creator of the universe. Second, it provides you with a new perspective concerning the events and experiences of your life. Religious imagery gives you the power to change the way you think, feel, and act. Reflecting and imagining in a religious context unleashes your creative gifts so they can work to heal and transform your life. Third, religious imagery helps you reconcile differences within your perception. While your intellect functions to separate and evaluate, your imagination works to unite and bring together internal conflicts.

In the prologue of *The Soul's Journey Into God*, Saint Bonaventure (1217-1274) states that we should not think that "reading is sufficient without unction, speculation without devotion, investigation without wonder, observation without joy, work without piety, knowledge without love, understanding without humility, endeavor without divine grace, reflection…without divinely inspired wisdom." Religious imagery achieves this goal by integrating these opposites so we can find a greater balance in our spiritual development.

It is impossible to compile a complete list of all the religious images that can be utilized in Fantasy Prayer. Images that are meaningful to some people do not touch others. Although the Bible is a rich source of religious images, it is not the sole source. At the same time, you cannot simply create a religious image by attaching God or Jesus to something secular. An image is religious because it manifests a particular aspect of God's care for you personally.

Some examples of religious images that have touched many people are: the Trinity, Holy Wisdom, Sophia, the Body of Christ, the Heart of Jesus, Jesus' Precious Blood, the Good Shepherd, the Living Water, the Bread of Life, the Light of God, and various images from the stories and parables in the gospels.

To use a religious image in Fantasy Prayer, you close your eyes and picture one of the images just listed. While you let relaxation and peace flow through your entire being, you become aware of the thoughts and feelings that the image brings to mind. Allow the image to bring you deeper and deeper within it and within God.

This type of prayer does not demand a great deal of activity. Simply allow the religious image or symbol to carry you along, and remain receptive to the ways God reveals divine love through this image. Be aware of the thoughts and feelings that are going on inside of you, and respond to the inspiration of the Spirit.

Some people find it difficult to concentrate on an image for a definite period of time. Others find that praying with religious images results in endless distractions. It is important to remember that most people have not been trained to pray in images and thus find it awkward when they first attempt this method of prayer. Through repetition and practice, however, you cannot only learn how to pray with religious images but also discover that this prayer style can be another path to closer union with God, personal healing, and spiritual growth.

While some people find it difficult to use Fantasy Prayer, other people find that God becomes immediately present to them in this prayer approach. Fantasy Prayer helped a young man who was having a hard time keeping a steady job. Everything he tried to do seemed doomed to failure. He was frustrated, discouraged, and afraid to even attempt another job interview. In prayer he visualized himself carrying a bright red worry bag. Each time he had a negative, fearful thought he put that thought into the worry bag and gave it to God saying, "I am letting go and letting God." As he repeated this prayer many times over a period of months, he began to feel a healing of his frustrations. He experienced a new trust in God's presence giving him the self-confidence he needed. Before long he found steady employment.

An elderly woman who had been a victim of child abuse and whose parents were alcoholics, also found healing through Fantasy Prayer. She had many painful memories of being left alone as a young child with no one to care for her. She also remembered how her parents, when they had too much to drink, would scream at her, beat her, or send her to her room without supper. Even though she had dealt with these memories long ago and now had a wonderful family of her own, she still felt occasional rootlessness and loneliness—like a deprived orphan.

Through Fantasy Prayer this woman was able to re-create the scene of her own birth. She imagined God the Creator tenderly holding this new daughter, softly speaking words of love to her, and protecting her with parental concern. She visualized Mary, the Mother of Jesus, cuddling and caressing her with a mother's love. As a result of this prayer, the woman came to feel loved and cherished as a special member of God's family. She decided to continue praying for healing, visualizing the Spirit as a mother bird taking her on strong wings to new places where she discovered hidden treasures within herself. This woman shared her experiences of healing with people who had undergone similar traumas, joined a support group of Adult Children of Alcoholics, and did volunteer work with child-abuse victims.

If you would like help getting started with Fantasy Prayer, consult *Quiet Places with Jesus* (Twenty-Third Publications, 1978) and *Quiet Places with Mary* (Twenty-Third Publications, 1986) by Rev. Isaias Powers, C.P. and *Sadhana: A Way to God* (Doubleday, 1984) by Anthony de Mello, S.J. The first two books contain guided imagery meditations dealing with painful topics like loneliness, depression, rejection, and anger. *Sadhana: A Way to God* contains eighteen beautiful fantasy prayers. All three books can be ordered through your local bookstore.

FANTASY PRAYER

Before trying this exercise, remember the difference between memory and fantasy. Memory recalls the past as you remember it; fantasy allows you to relive the event in a new way. In fantasy, you are no longer aware of your present environment. You are actually living in your fantasy place. If you are on a deserted island near the ocean, you see the storm-tossed waves, hear the roar of the ocean, and feel the wind blowing through your hair.

You may want to choose a suitable musical selection to enhance your Fantasy Prayer. It is best to use a classical instrumental piece that will match the mood of the meditation.

If you use this prayer experience in a small group, be sure to allow sufficient time for all participants to get in touch with their thoughts and feelings. A series of dots (…) indicates a pause of several minutes during which participants can enter prayerful reflection.

After selecting a quiet place, begin this prayer with a relaxation exercise.

PRAYER

Close your eyes and pay attention to your breathing…As you inhale, breathe in healing love…peacefulness…compassion…As you exhale, breathe out all negative thoughts…tensions…resentments…anger…
Quietly remain aware of your breathing for a while…

In your imagination go to a deserted island…Hear and see the waves crashing wildly against the sandy beach…Hear and feel the wind blowing fiercely…Note that a storm is blowing in off the water…You are alone…You begin to feel lonely and frightened…You remember all the people in your life who have abandoned you…You remember a recent time when you grieved a major loss in your life…Feel once again the sadness, anger, fear, and loneliness that this experience created within you…

Gradually, notice that you are not, in fact, alone on your deserted island...Someone is walking toward you...You recognize that it is God...God comes toward you...takes your hand...leads you to a sheltered cave...There, sheltered from the wind and the storm, share your lonely experience with God...

As the storm begins to die down, slowly leave the cave behind, and walk with God along the beach...Together, wonder at the golden-red sunset...the graceful sea gulls overhead...the powerful movement of the waves across the sand...

After time spent in quiet sharing, God gives you a gift...God tells you that this gift is a special treasure that has been created for you...Hold this treasure to your heart as a reminder of God's presence with you...

God gently embraces you...As you hold your treasure to your heart, watch God stroll off down the beach...Feel God's presence remain with you in the treasure...Notice how your sadness, anger, fear, and loneliness seem to have lost their strength...

 **FURTHER REFLECTION**

INDIVIDUAL

How did God speak to me in a special way through Fantasy Prayer?

How did I experience healing in this encounter with God?

When has a religious image revealed God's love to me in a special way? What feelings did I have during that experience?

What negative thought patterns would I like to have healed?

Are there hurtful situations or memories that I would like to see in a new light? Can Fantasy Prayer help me do this?

How has my relationship with God changed as a result of my experience of Fantasy Prayer?

GROUP

How can Fantasy Prayer help us experience God's healing in a deeper way?

Albert Schweitzer said, "The greatest discovery of any generation is that human beings can alter their lives by altering their attitudes of mind." Do we agree? disagree? Why?

Why do negative thoughts become stumbling blocks that keep us from using our unique gifts?

How can Fantasy Prayer be used to change negative thoughts so we can experience freedom and healing?

What are some of our favorite religious images? How can using religious imagery in prayer foster our spiritual growth as individuals and as a community?

RELAXATION PRAYER

"Oh, I had such a stressful day. The children fought constantly. I didn't think we'd make it through dinner."

"I often work eleven-hour days. If I stay at home when one of the kids is sick, I have to work a weekend or stay until nine or ten o'clock at night. The boss just keeps piling extra duties on me because our company is downsizing."

"I'm so tired of all the rushing around I have to do. There is never enough hours in the day to get everything done. I just want to get away from it all."

Sound familiar? Those of us who live busy lives often feel like we're on a treadmill. The fact is, balancing family, job, and other responsibilities in today's complicated world is tough.

As a result, stress appears to be epidemic. In a recent national survey of five hundred working women, nearly half of the women surveyed complained that their jobs had become more stressful in the past five years. (The results of the survey, conducted by EDK Associates, a research firm in New York, appeared in "Same Job, Less Stress" by Leslie Laurence, *Redbook*, November 1994, p. 75.) Ironically, when we seek relief from our stress, we often engage in more activities that exhaust us further.

Our negative thoughts and emotions contribute to our level of stress. Fear, worry, anxiety, high blood pressure, ulcers, and headaches are symptoms of stress that affect our physical and emotional well-being. If only we could relax and let go of the tension that saps our energy and drains our enthusiasm.

We don't have to look far to find a variety of solutions to this problem. Bookstores, newspaper stands, cassette and video tapes, and workshops offer a wide variety of experiences and material on how to manage—even minimize—our stress level. Much of this material focuses on eating well, getting adequate rest, massage therapy, and other relaxation techniques.

Relaxation Prayer is a reliable means of handling stress. Helping us get in touch with our spiritual center, this prayer approach shows us how to turn over our stresses to God and to discover God's loving presence. Relaxation Prayer allows us to realize that God is with us, everywhere and always, in the midst of our busy lives: in our relationships, activities, joys, hopes, disappointments, fears, and anxieties. God loves each of us totally, completely, passionately, and personally, as if we were the only person in the universe. The Holy One is as close to us as the air we breathe. All we have to do is open ourselves to the powerful healing presence of God who wants to free us from stress and help us become whole and holy.

Understanding Relaxation Prayer

In Relaxation Prayer, you open yourself to God's presence dwelling within you. You get in touch with that quiet strength and timeless wisdom that is God. In the depths of your heart, you wait and listen for God. You maintain an attitude of attentive waiting while God draws you near. You release the distractions of the day that cause stress and tension, and let yourself go into God's love.

Relaxation Prayer draws upon your imagination to guide you. Some people can easily engage all the senses—sight, taste, touch, sound, and smell—to experience a scene rich with reality. Other people do not see or experience anything, but have a "sense" of the scene imagined. When I use this prayer approach, I usually get only a vague glimpse of the scene, but I have a real sense of being there. The important thing to remember is that when you use your imagination in prayer, you open a profound channel for God's healing power to enter your life.

When you bring your Relaxation Prayer to a close, be gentle with yourself. Before moving away from your prayer time, rest in the mystery of Divine Love. Be conscious of any thoughts, images, feelings, or insights that emerge. You may want to record these in a prayer journal.

There are a variety of approaches to relax the body and renew the spirit with Relaxation Prayer. The following models will help you let go of fatigue and stress and sink into the embrace of healing love.

 RELAXATION PRAYER

Preparation for Relaxation Prayer is especially important. Although the purpose of Relaxation Prayer is to help you bring

your stress and tensions into a prayerful presence before God,
you must approach this prayer with some measure of calm.
Spend several minutes relaxing your body and calming your
mind. Do some physical stretching, deep breathing exercises,
or any technique that helps you become silent and recollected
in body and spirit.

If you use this prayer experience in a small group, be sure to
allow sufficient time for all participants to get in touch with
their thoughts and feelings. A series of dots (…) indicates a
pause of several minutes during which participants can enter
prayerful reflection. Pauses and environment are especially
important in this model of prayer. Where a pause is noted, be
sure to allow sufficient time, and enhance your prayer
atmosphere with classical or instrumental music.

Before beginning your prayer, read the prayer suggestions
several times. Then close your eyes, and repeat the main ideas
to yourself. Don't worry about getting everything exactly right.
Follow your own inner guidance, and focus on the ideas that
draw you more deeply into the Divine Presence. You may
want to record Relaxation Prayer on a cassette, with music in
the background. Once again, be sure to allow long pauses for
your response.

RELAXING IN LOVE

In a comfortable position, become aware of your
body…Focus on your tense or tight muscles…Moving
from the top of your head to the bottom of your feet,
alternately tighten and release the muscles in each area of
your body…

Notice any physical discomfort…Put your hand on any
tense or tight muscles…Become aware as you do so that
the healing hand of God is touching you with gentleness

and compassion…Feel the tension leave your body…Observe Infinite Love freeing you…healing you…filling you…renewing you…with new energy for living and loving…

Be aware of your emotions…Feel them…Don't try to judge or change them, simply acknowledge them…Recall recent times of joy…sadness…fear…anxiety…As you recall each feeling, release it to the Holy One…Give yourself and all your emotions to God…

Reflect on your life as a journey into the infinite depths of Divine Love…Give thanks for the times you have experienced this deep love…

Rejoice in God's extravagant love for you…Ask God to love you now as you have never been loved before— beyond your expectations and wildest dreams…Be open to wonderful surprises…

Contemplate the richness and beauty of this boundless love…Rest for as long as you can in this unfathomable mystery of Divine Love…

Be aware of the ways God is working through you at this time to share Divine Love with others…Praise God for these opportunities…

Be aware of any feelings that emerge as you reflect on God's infinite love…Ask God to help you be more receptive to Eternal Love, now and always…

Gently become aware of your surroundings, and bring your prayer to a quiet close…

REJOICING IN GOD'S EMBRACE

Breathe deeply and slowly, allowing your diaphragm to expand and contract…Slowly count to five each time you breathe in and each time you breathe out…Do this for several minutes until you feel relaxed…

Imagine that you are at your favorite nature spot: the ocean, the mountains, by a lake, in a meadow, at a park, in the woods…The sky is clear and blue…The sun feels warm…There is a gentle breeze…

Lie down on the earth and take a sun bath…The warm and gentle rays of the sun embrace you…The beauty of creation fills you with awe and wonder…

Now, hear someone coming…Open your eyes, and see God walking toward you…Slowly, gently, respectfully, God embraces you with overwhelming and unconditional love…God's arms hold you close to the divine heart…

Relax in God's embrace for as long as you wish…

God shares with you a personal message of deep love that frees, heals, renews, and strengthens you…Delight in God's wondrous love for you…Experience the peace and joy that are yours…

God asks you to be a reflection of divine, healing love to others, especially certain individuals…Share with God the challenges you think you will encounter as you strive to lovingly serve the needs of these people…Name, affirm, and thank God for each of the special gifts you bring to your ministry to others…

Observe God's love acting powerfully in your life now…Get in touch with your feelings of joy, happiness, peace, enthusiasm…

Gently become aware of your surroundings, and bring your prayer to a quiet close…

EXPERIENCING GOD'S PEACE

Sit in a comfortable position, or lay flat on the floor or in your bed…Let yourself relax…

Breathe in deeply through your nose and exhale through your mouth…Breathe in energy and peace…Exhale tension and stress…Your face feels relaxed…as you let go of all tension…Your neck and back feel relaxed…as you let go of all tension…Your chest and stomach feel relaxed…as you let go of all tension…Your arms and legs feel relaxed…as you let go of all tension…

Imagine yourself walking in a lush, green mountain meadow…The air is fresh and clear…The scent of the tall majestic pines that border the meadow fills the air…The sky is blue and the sun is bright…A gentle breeze caresses your body…Watch the fluffy white clouds as they float effortlessly by…You are surrounded by a beautiful array of yellow, pink, purple, and red wildflowers…Breathe deeply…As you stroll, you pause to smell, touch, and admire the flowers…the trees…the plants…the birds…

Find a shady spot near a tree, and sit or lay down…Close your eyes…Journey deep within your being, to your center…See there a golden light glowing brightly…This loving energy flows to every cell of your body…Sense that you are in the presence of the tender warmth of

God's powerful love for you…Experience a love that is beyond all telling and a vibrant joy that cannot be expressed…In this wonderful place of heavenly love, relax completely…Discover inner calm, serenity, and deep peace…Recognize the new energy and life that fill your being…Become aware of ways you can be an instrument of God's peace in your everyday life…

Gently become aware of your surroundings, and bring your prayer to a quiet close…

 FURTHER REFLECTION

INDIVIDUAL

Where do I experience stress and anxiety in my life? What are the sources of my anxiety and stress?

How can I manage stress more effectively?

What are my favorite ways of relaxing?

How can prayer be a resource for me in dealing with stress and anxiety?

GROUP

How does our culture deal with stress?

What are healthy ways of managing stress and anxiety in ordinary life?

What are some spiritual resources that can be used in stress management?

What impact could these spiritual resources have on our culture's approach to stress management?

How is Relaxation Prayer an effective tool for dealing with stress?

HEALING AFFIRMATIONS *for* DAILY LIVING

Affirmations or healing words can be powerful tools for spiritual growth. Such words help us move forward in spite of our fears, and enable us to let go of past failures. Affirmations put us in touch with the divine wisdom that dwells deep within each of us.

Affirmations are positive, repeated thoughts that have the power to transform our beliefs and attitudes. In his book, *Words That Heal: Affirmations and Meditations for Daily Living* (Bantam Books, 1990), Douglas Bloch explains that affirmations are based on the following principles:

- Our outer reality is a manifestation of our predominate beliefs and thoughts.
- When we change our beliefs, we change our attitudes.
- Our thoughts and beliefs are reflected through the written and spoken word.

I recall a difficult situation at work that threatened the principles of justice and equality for all that I cherish. To quiet my fears and keep myself calm I created the following affirmation: "I rejoice that God's power is transforming this situation now." As I repeated these words over and over again I began to experience a sense of peace that permeated my entire being. In that process, I discovered the courage I needed to join with others to work for change.

We can use affirmations to heal our minds and emotions by focusing on a positive belief, value, or attitude. Words have a creative life-giving power that can bring healing and spiritual growth to ourselves and others. Consider affirmations such as: "The love of God embraces me," "God is loving and healing me now," "I let go and let God," "My life overflows with the goodness of God," "My heart is filled with compassion," and "The presence of God is always with me." These words strengthen our spirits and generate a loving awareness of God's intimate presence.

Understanding Healing Affirmations for Daily Living

There are several approaches to finding the affirmations that minister to your own unique needs. Review the following model as one effective means of "composing" your own healing affirmation.

Choose an area in your life that needs healing or growth. You can create affirmations that deal with a wide array of life's challenges, such as your relationships (with yourself, your spouse, your friends, your neighbors, God), health or financial concerns, job stresses, grief or loss issues, and so forth. Where do you hurt? Your body, mind, emotions, and spirit reveal your deepest needs; listen to them.

Decide what changes this healing would bring to your life. Ask yourself, *How would my life be different if I were to experience healing in this area, relationship, or situation? What feelings would I experience if this were to occur?* In the example here, you let go of resentment, and experience peace and confidence in yourself.

Writing in the first person, compose a positive statement that expresses your desire for healing. Make sure your affirmation states exactly what you need, the deepest desire of your heart. "I release my anger and am filled with peace." "I let go of resentment and let God fill me with peace." "I can do all things in the power of God within me." "I am confident and open to new and wonderful opportunities." "I am confident and peaceful." Be willing to write several possibilities before you discover the affirmation that is right for you.

Repeat your affirmation often. Repeating the affirmation reinforces positive beliefs and thought patterns that bring healing. When you repeat the words "I am confident and peaceful," for example, you become confident and peaceful. When you repeat the words "I let go of resentment and let God fill me with peace," you experience the healing presence of God's love acting powerfully in your life.

Once you've developed your own healing affirmations, consider placing written copies of them where you will see them often: on the refrigerator door, the bathroom mirror, the dashboard of the car. You might want to create an affirmation journal in which you record your affirmations and the thoughts, feelings, insights, and perceptions that you experience. Some people record their affirmations on a cassette and play them back first thing in the morning, throughout the day, and/or in the evening before retiring. Do what feels comfortable so you can experience the healing and spiritual growth which is God's will for you.

Although your prayer affirmations may be limited since God alone sees the whole picture, you can have confidence that God is always working in every situation, relationship, and event of your life. Your prayers will be answered in God's time and in ways that surpass your greatest expectations. "Eye has not seen, ear has not heard, / ...what God has prepared for those who love..." (1 Corinthians 2:9).

HEALING AFFIRMATIONS FOR DAILY LIVING

Before you begin using healing affirmations, get in touch with how powerful words can be, how they can wound, how they can heal. Ask yourself, What do I talk about? What do I say? Do I engage in negative self-talk or do I allow words to help me live up to my potential? Do I make positive statements about myself and others or am I negative and judgmental? If you experience problems with your health, relationships, finances, or job, or if you struggle with grief or loss, or if you seek encouragement and support, the following healing affirmation exercises can offer you insight and strength. These healing words invite you to experience the immensity of God's love for you in a powerful new way, bringing you fresh hope for healing and spiritual growth.

If you use this prayer experience in a small group, be sure to allow sufficient time for all participants to get in touch with their thoughts and feelings. A series of dots (...) indicates a pause of several minutes during which participants can enter prayerful reflection.

THE SPIRIT OF GOD BREATHES IN ME

Sit or lie down in a comfortable position and close your eyes...Become aware of your body...Allow your consciousness to focus on each part of the body so that you can relax fully...Become aware of relaxation flowing through your head...your hair...your eyes...your ears...your face...

Become aware of relaxation flowing through your neck...your shoulders...your arms...your hands...

Become aware of the clothes on your body...Feel your clothes touching the surface of your skin...

Become aware of relaxation flowing through your chest...your stomach...your back...your hips...your genitals...your legs...

Relax your mind, and let go of all thoughts and images...Let stray thoughts and images float in and out effortlessly...Let your mind go blank...

Let go of any outside noises or distractions...Let go of everything...

Become aware that all tension is gone...Become aware of your own deep peacefulness...Note how your feelings come and go like the waves of the ocean...

Become aware of your breathing...Listen to it...Feel your chest rise and fall...Feel the cool air enter your nostrils and fill your lungs...Feel the warm air flow from your lungs and through your nostrils...Breathe deeply so that the diaphragm rises when you breathe in and lowers when you breathe out...

Become aware that the Holy Spirit, the Breath of God, breathes in you...God's breath fills you with a wonderful sense of well-being, healing, energy, freedom, and joy...Breathe in God's Spirit, and relax fully in the Breath of Life...Breathe out God's Spirit to everyone and to all creation...

(Choose one or more of the following Prayer Affirmations, or create your own, and repeat for several minutes. Breathe in the words of the first part of the affirmation, and breathe out the words of the second part.)

Breathe in	Breathe out
God's Spirit	breathes in me.
God's Spirit	heals me.
God's Spirit	frees me.
God's Spirit	empowers me.
God's Spirit	transforms me.
I am	the Breath of God *(select one or more)* to my spouse, friends, children, neighbors, church, world, creation.

Conclude your prayer time by writing your prayer affirmation and posting it in a prominent place as a reminder to repeat it often. You may want to express your response to your affirmation or express your affirmation in some creative way such as poetry, song, dance, art, or crafts.

AFFIRMING SELF AND OTHERS

Relax and be still...Inhale God's healing love...Exhale any negative thoughts or feelings...Inhale the healing energy that God wants you to experience...Imagine healing love flowing through your body, mind, emotions, and will...

In your imagination, invite different people to emerge one at a time...Look into each person's eyes...Be aware of each person's sacred uniqueness...Thank God for the blessings you have received through each person...

Picture yourself affirming others in your prayer each day...Open yourself to the blessings that specific people are for you, such as your spouse, children, parents, relatives, coworkers, boss, neighbors, members of your faith community...Experience the love that God is pouring out to you through them...Express your appreciation to each person in a deeply personal and loving manner...

(Think of a specific person, then choose one or more of the following Prayer Affirmations or create your own. Repeat for several minutes.)

- I praise God for your goodness.
- I praise God for your strength.
- I praise God for your compassion.
- I praise God for your joy.
- I thank God for you.
- I hold you in my heart.
- I experience joy in your presence.
- I experience peace in your presence.
- I experience confidence in your presence.
- I encounter Divine Love through you.

Imagine others affirming you...Hear a specific person tell you something positive about yourself...Listen carefully, and feel your spirit lighten...

(Think of a specific person, then choose one or more of the following Prayer Affirmations or create your own. Repeat for several minutes.)

- You are important to me.
- My life is better because of you.
- I appreciate the person you are.
- You do good work.
- I enjoy sharing my life with you.

Imagine yourself talking to your reflection in a mirror… Note your facial features…Study your eyes…Smile at yourself…Consider yourself as a precious person…

(Choose one of the following self-worth Prayer Affirmations, or create your own. Repeat as often as possible.)

- I value myself.
- I am created in God's image.
- I have something unique to offer others.
- I take good care of myself.
- I am a radiant reflection of God's love.
- I am an instrument of Divine Love.

Recall times when you reached out in loving service to others…Offer thanks for these opportunities to love and grow…

Recall times when others ministered lovingly to your needs…Offer thanks for these opportunities to love and grow…

Decide on practical ways you can affirm your own worth and the dignity of others, especially those with whom you live and work…

ANGEL WORDS REVEAL DIVINE LOVE

Relax in any position...Imagine that you are at the ocean, lying on the beach with your feet in the water...Hear the crashing of the waves, and feel the coolness of the water creep up over you, cleansing your body as it washes over you gently...Each wave fills you with joy...Rest as long as you can on the beach...

Notice a beautiful white light coming toward you...Sense that someone who loves you is approaching...Recognize an angel walking toward you...Let the angel take your hand and lift you gently onto her wings...Feel the secure warmth of her nearness...Feel her raise you up over the ocean...higher...into the clouds...

Slowly, gracefully, slip from the angel's wings...Dance among the clouds, from one to the other...Look down on the blue, foaming waters thousands of feet below...As you play with your angel friend, notice the sparkling light that radiates around you and fills you with healing love...Feel the new energy that washes over your body...Become aware of new insights into the infinite depths of God's love for you...Feel the wonder of your own goodness...

Hear your angel reveal to you a special message from God...You understand that these healing words will transform your life forever...Pause and repeat these words to yourself...Write these words in the clouds...As you do so, feel a lightness of heart...Give thanks for the wonderful experience of the breadth and length and height and depth of God's love for you...

Remain among the clouds with your angel friend for as long as you want...

(Choose one of the following prayerful affirmations or create your own "angel words." Repeat these affirmations often during your day as reminders of God's love for you.)

- I expect miracles to occur in my life.
- My life overflows with every kind of blessing.
- I let go of my fears and trust God completely.
- I clothe myself with the glory of God.
- All things are working together for good in my life.
- My body is healed and filled with love.

 **FURTHER REFLECTION**

INDIVIDUAL

From whom and in what ways have I experienced affirmation or positive strokes in my life?

How have I grown from giving and receiving affirmation?

How important are compliments in my daily life?

How can Healing Affirmation Prayer help me experience God's presence in myself and others?

GROUP

How does contemporary society deal with the need for affirmation?

How can affirmations or healing words help us grow spiritually?

In what ways can we express appreciation for the goodness of others?

How can we, as Christians, use affirmation to build up our faith community?

In what ways can Healing Affirmation Prayer be a resource for individuals and families in times of crisis or struggle?

PRAYER *for* HEALING FAMILIES, RACES, NATIONS, RELIGIONS, *and* EARTH

Five-year-old Katie was sitting on the couch, staring at her hands, thinking, an unusual posture for a young lady who enjoyed chatter, games of imagination, and storytelling.

"What are you thinking about Katie?" I asked.

"I'm thinking about that big fight Danny and I had today. I really didn't mean to hit him so hard, but he pulled my hair. I told him I was sorry."

"Is there anything you'd like to say to Danny?"

"Yeah," Katie said, jumping up and running over to where her two-year-old brother, Danny, was playing. "I really love you—no matter what."

All of us experience tension and conflict in our daily interactions. We want to love and be loved, but the stresses and strains of modern living sometimes prevent us from loving one another as well as we would like. All of us need healing in our relationships if we are to "really love—no matter what," as Katie said.

The conflict among families, races, religions, nations, and the environmental degradation of Earth is like a slow growing cancer destroying the heart of all life. We are God's children, members of a spiritual family, who are deeply connected with one another and share a common home: Earth. We need to find effective ways to cast out the demons of racism, discrimination, abuse, and violence in our world and be healers of both human hearts and our home, Earth.

Our contemporary resources are not sufficient to stem the growth of violence and hatred in our streets and around the world. Only God can accomplish such a gigantic task. Our prayers, however, are powerful ways for us to bring healing in our homes, on our streets, in our churches and synagogues, between people of different races and nations, and to Earth. When we pray we bring to God our relationships with family, friends, neighbors, strangers, and peoples of different races, religions, and nations. Prayer enables us to transform our lives and our world. Through God's grace, people are cleansed and healed each day. Through prayer and meditation we grow more deeply conscious of our role as good stewards of creation, a creation that reflects the glorious face of God in our midst. (See Genesis 1:28-30.)

Through prayer we expand our consciousness to realize that God is Love, and when we love we give birth to that powerful and mysterious energy that makes miracles happen. "Beloved, let us love one another, because love is of God; everyone who loves is born of God and knows God....God is love… (1 John 4:7,16).

Understanding Prayer for Healing Families, Races, Nations, Religions, and Earth

Prayer for Healing Families, Races, Nations, Religions, and Earth asks God to heal the conflicts and pain that damage all that is critical to our survival and happiness. The following examples represent prayers of healing for the family and prayers of release from the darkness of discrimination and injustice that traumatize people of different races, religions, and nations. Also, there is a prayer for Earth's healing.

To open ourselves to the passionate, healing love of God that fills us with deep peace, surpasses all our dreams for intimacy, restores our hope, and transforms our world, we must humbly acknowledge the pain and brokenness that surround us. We need only touch our immediate world to know that pain.

PRAYER FOR HEALING FAMILIES, RACES, NATIONS, RELIGIONS, AND EARTH

If you use this prayer experience in a small group, be sure to allow sufficient time for all participants to get in touch with their thoughts and feelings. A series of dots (…) indicates a pause of several minutes during which participants can enter prayerful reflection.

HEALING PRAYER FOR FAMILY RELATIONSHIPS

Relax…Take several deep breaths…Beginning at the top of the head, slowly relax every part of your body…Close your eyes…

Go back to your childhood…Recall those times when you felt loved by members of your family…Pay attention to your feelings…Experience the sights, sounds, tastes, and aromas…Remember how people looked…how you felt…Remember the places where these loving encounters took place…Savor the warmth of these happy times for as long as possible…

In your imagination, share your positive feelings with each family member…Look into each one's eyes, and express your appreciation for the love you experienced…

Be aware of each one's reaction to your loving words…

Recall times when you experienced misunderstandings, hurt, confusion, or anger in your relationships with your family…Ask God to help you "want to want" to forgive your family for their failures…Imagine God's forgiveness flowing over the hurt places in your heart and healing you…See the hurtful situations and painful relationships of the past as opportunities of grace where God was present and loving you…Open yourself to divine compassion welling up inside you…

Recall those times when you have failed to love fully…Become aware of any need you may have to forgive yourself for your failures to love members of your family…Be aware that sometimes you expect more of yourself in your relationships than God does…Ask God to forgive and heal you…Allow God's boundless love to saturate your entire being and fill you with peace…

Be aware of times in which your failure to love caused pain, disappointment, anger, frustration, or anxiety in your family…In your imagination, go to each person and ask forgiveness for your past failures…Express your desire to be a channel of God's love to each person…Ask, "What can I do to love you more deeply now?"…Invite God to reveal to you new ways that you can be a blessing to your family now…

As you bring your prayer to a close, write your thoughts, desires, and feelings about these relationships in a prayer journal and/or in a love letter to each family member. Consider planning a special celebration or surprise that your family members will enjoy such as a reunion, vacation, party, or surprise visit.

HEALING PRAYER FOR RACES, NATIONS, AND RELIGIONS

Stand up, stretch, and take some deep breaths…Now sit down, close your eyes, and gently journey to the center of your being…Open yourself to God's presence creating a new world on Earth…Be aware of God's power working now to remove the walls that separate people from one another…Be conscious that the Divine plan for the world is peace, justice, and love…

Slowly read the following Scripture:

> *They shall beat their swords into plowshares*
> *   and their spears into pruning hooks;*
> *One nation shall not raise the sword against another,*
> *   nor shall they train for war again.*
> *O house of Jacob, come,*
> *   let us walk in the light of the Lord!*

Isaiah 2:4-5

Repeat as a prayer phrase or mantra: "Come, let us walk together in justice and peace…"

Imagine God creating harmony and peace between races, religions, and nations throughout the world...As you pray, realize that God is acting powerfully to make the divine vision a reality now...Ponder the mystery that all people dwell together in love in the Heart of God...

Observe races giving and receiving forgiveness... Caucasians, African Americans, Hispanics, Asian Americans, Native Americans...Join in their prayer for deep healing of prejudices that besiege the human heart...Join in their prayer for the transformation of policies and structures that support discrimination and racism...Join in their prayer for liberation: "Come, let us walk together in justice and peace..."

Imagine Serbs, Croatians, and Bosnians giving and receiving forgiveness...Observe Jews and Arabs embracing in the Holy Land...Observe Protestants and Catholics in Northern Ireland rebuilding their troubled nation...Observe all South Africans living together in harmony...

Observe past generations and future generations joining together, acknowledging the evils of the past, casting out the demons of hatred and violence, and living together in peace as God's children...

Imagine God's forgiveness enabling a miraculous healing to occur between nations, ethnic groups, and religions...Pray for healing: "Come, let us walk together in justice and peace..."

Observe representatives from any conflicting groups sitting in a circle...Imagine one representative at a time getting up, walking to the other representatives, and asking for forgiveness for the cruelty and wrongs done by his or her group to the members of the other groups in the circle…Smile at the warmth and tenderness of this exchange…Imagine the group holding hands and praying silently…Join their circle, and pray for spiritual unity and community among all God's people: "Come, let us walk together in justice and peace…"

Observe all races, nations, and religions living together in peace, love, and justice…Imagine all people working together as sisters and brothers for the common good of the human family…Observe tender mercy, fresh hope, and boundless compassion breaking forth everywhere among all people…Pray for this transformation of the human heart: "Come, let us walk together in justice and peace…"

HEALING PRAYER FOR EARTH

Become aware of your breathing…As you breathe in, become aware of the warm air flowing through your nostrils and filling your lungs…As you breathe out, release any anxiety or worry…

Take a walk or simply gaze out the window at your favorite nature scene…With all your senses, observe the beauty of creation…Contemplate the skies…the sun…the clouds…the moon…the stars…the trees…the plants…the flowers…Hear the voices of the gentle breeze…the brilliant thunder…the singing birds speaking a special message…Simply "be" with God's creatures… Contemplate your connectedness with Earth…

Listen to the cry of Earth in air…in water…in forests…in rivers, as she reveals to you one of the great tragedies of our time: environmental degradation…Ask Earth to forgive you for your ignorance…for your lack of appreciation…for your neglect and/or abuse of her resources…for excessive consumerism…Be aware of how you can help heal Earth and be healed by Earth…

Ask Earth to forgive society for polluting air and water…endangering animal and plant life…cutting and burning the rain forests…overconsuming natural resources…causing soil erosion…creating toxic and solid waste dumping…depleting the ozone layer…Be aware of how society can help heal Earth and be healed by Earth…

Be aware that all creation is in need of salvation, not just human beings…Imagine all "creation awaits with eager expectation for the revelation of the children of God" and that "all creation is groaning in labor pains even until now" (Romans 8:19,22)…

As you bring your prayer to a close, consider (or imagine yourself) kissing the earth, hugging a tree, sitting on the grass, rolling in the snow, walking in the rain, dancing in the moonlight, climbing a tree, or doing something creative and fun to celebrate and bless Earth. Draw or make a symbol that will keep Earth's beauty present to you. Consider becoming more self-sustaining. Grow your own vegetables, bake bread, collect rain water in a barrel for watering outdoor and indoor plants, sew a garment, create pottery cookware. You may want to support or join a group that lobbies for policies, programs, and laws that will heal our bioregion and support ecojustice.

# FURTHER REFLECTION

INDIVIDUAL

How can prayer heal my relationships with others?

How can I grow from giving and receiving forgiveness?

In what ways can I work for the healing of races, nations, and religions?

How can I be healed by Earth and be a healer of Earth?

GROUP

How can healing prayer help families grow spiritually?

How can healing prayer promote greater cooperation, understanding, and unity among races, nations, and religions?

In what ways can changing our way of life and simplifying our lifestyles make a contribution to ecojustice?

How do environmental action groups effect change in laws, policies, and structures that will impact Earth's healing? In what ways can we grow spiritually by joining groups that work for ecojustice?

PRAYER *of* THE SUFFERER

Several years ago, Jeannie was diagnosed with cancer. She spent a year in radiation and chemotherapy. While her family and friends were supportive and prayed for Jeannie's healing, her condition deteriorated. Finally, her doctor told her that the tumor was growing and there was nothing that could be done.

Jeannie called me and wanted to talk. As we sipped tea, she poured out her pain and frustration. "Why me? Why do I have to suffer so much pain? Why doesn't God answer our prayers for healing?"

We all ask this question when pain enters our lives directly: "Why me?" I had no answers for Jeannie, just as Jesus had no answer to the question of human suffering or unanswered prayer. Nobody wants pain, but it is there throughout all of life. Jesus showed us that God is one with us in our suffering and in our pain, and that Divine Love transforms human suffering. When we join our sufferings to Christ, we help redeem the world. By his Cross and Resurrection, Jesus showed us how to live with suffering and pain: let go and let God. "Jesus cried out in a loud voice, 'Father, into your hands I commend my spirit;' and when he had said this he breathed his last" (Luke 23:44).

None of our pain is wasted. Jesus loves us so much that he takes all our life's pain to the Cross with him, and there it becomes salvific for us and for all humanity. When we take up our cross and follow Christ, our sufferings become part of God's plan for the redemption of the world. Our pain gives hope and courage to all people who suffer. We have been supported in our own suffering through the sufferings and prayers of our relatives, friends, the communion of the saints, and all those who have gone before us. One day we will see these blessed saints who have loved us so much.

Understanding Prayer of the Sufferer

In times of disappointment and sadness, you become open to seeking God's assistance because you realize that you cannot make it on your own. A meaningful relationship is terminated, some opportunity you wanted becomes unavailable, a job promotion creates more problems than you anticipated, a financial problem threatens your financial security, your children reject the values and faith that you treasure, your heart is broken because of loss or separation from loved ones: these situations put you in touch with your own helplessness, and you turn to God.

When things like this occur you need not despair. You know that God is present: "I am with you always, to the end of the age" (Matthew 28:20). In moments when you experience loss and pain, or when your prayers seem to go unanswered, you grow spiritually.

In the summer of 1973 my father was diagnosed with a severe case of pancreatitis. The doctor told us all we could do was pray. At that time I was stationed in

Philadelphia and traveled back and forth to Virginia on weekends to be with my family. Each time I visited Dad in the hospital and saw him hooked up to intravenous tubes, I felt so helpless. It was painful to sit by his bedside, hold his hand, and be unable to do anything to alleviate his suffering. It was painful to see the sadness in my mother's eyes. It was painful to realize that Dad couldn't be there to see his son, Sean, play on the high school football team or to help his other son, Patrick, deal with the challenges of young adulthood. It seemed that when we needed Dad most, we were going to lose him.

As the months went by, Dad grew worse. I remember one unusually chilly night in November when I returned to Philadelphia after visiting Dad and my family; I was exhausted. I knelt by my bed and poured out my heart to God, crying, arguing, bargaining, expressing my anger and frustration about the situation. Then suddenly, I heard an inner response: "Don't you know that I love your father far more than you do? I will take infinitely better care of him than you could possibly imagine."

At that moment I was able to let go and surrender Dad into God's loving embrace. I was filled with an awareness that God would do the best thing for Dad. A huge burden was lifted from me, and for the first time in months I felt deep peace. When negative thoughts and fears returned to threaten my serenity, I reminded myself to let go and let God take perfect care of Dad. After six months Dad slowly began to recover, and our family rejoiced that Dad was well again.

God loves, heals, and transforms you and your world through your suffering and pain. When things don't go according to your plans, when you experience disappointment and pain, when God doesn't seem to answer your prayers, you can surrender your pain to God and experience new life. When you suffer, God shares your every tear, fear, and pain. You can join your suffering to Christ and discover Love embracing you and transforming your life.

Sometimes God has a far greater gift of deep healing for you than you could imagine. You can look forward expectantly to the good that awaits you as God embraces you with love. No matter what happens in your life, even suffering, you can be confident that in the end, all will be well. "We know that all things work for good for those who love God, who are called according to [God's] purpose" (Romans 8:28).

Prayer helps you bring your sufferings into the heart of God. There you can let go and let God embrace you in your tears, pain, illnesses, losses, disappointments, and weaknesses. There you discover infinite, boundless, passionate Love calming your fears and assuring you that in every circumstance God is fully present. There you encounter God's saving power acting in your life in the midst of unanswered questions and puzzling mysteries. There you meet God dwelling in your spiritual depths.

PRAYER OF THE SUFFERER

The reflections in this section invite you to let go and let God in times of suffering, and to release obsessive, addictive, unhealthy, or broken relationships into God's loving care.

If you use this prayer experience in a small group, be sure to allow sufficient time for all participants to get in touch with their thoughts and feelings. A series of dots (…) indicates a pause of several minutes during which participants can enter prayerful reflection.

LETTING-GO-AND-LETTING-GOD PRAYER

Breathe slowly several times...Become aware of each breath as you inhale and exhale...Be aware of any tense areas in your body...Relax this tension by breathing God's healing love into these areas of stress...Continue breathing deeply until your body feels relaxed...Become completely still...

Pray the prayer of Jesus from the Cross: "Father, into your hands I commend my spirit"...Pray it again...Pray it again...

Imagine that you are standing by the cross of Jesus... Listen to Jesus' words...Imagine how Jesus feels...Imagine what you might say...Imagine what you might do... Imagine what you might feel...Imagine what you might think...Be aware of any images or insights that emerge as you encounter Jesus on the Cross...

Reflect on times during your life when you experienced loss...heartache...disappointment...loneliness... rejection...alienation...fear...anxiety...Remember those times when your prayers were not answered...Recall occasions when you were ill or in pain...when you felt lonely...helpless...isolated...depressed...Ask Jesus to embrace you as you remember these sufferings...

Become aware of ways that you grew during these experiences...Get in touch with lessons learned...insights discovered...values found...Become aware of ways that God is inviting you to grow now as you reflect on these experiences...In a loving conversation with God, express your thoughts and feelings about these occurrences...

Reflect on times you have experienced the power of Jesus' Death and Resurrection when you were sick…Be aware of the comfort and strength that Jesus' presence gave you, even if your pain or illness continued…As you recall these experiences, offer thanks for Jesus' love during these times…

Be aware of the "lepers" in your life, the difficult persons or experiences, the brokenness or pain, that you would rather ignore or avoid…Choose one of these persons or experiences to embrace…As you do so, imagine that this "leper" is the crucified Christ…Ask the Spirit to pray within you for the deepest needs of this person's heart…

Be aware of loved ones who are suffering…As each one comes to mind, imagine God embracing him or her with a love beyond all imagination…Pray the following verse over and over as a mantra for strength for each one: "We know that all things work for good for those who love God" (Romans 8:28)…Imagine Jesus taking each person's tears, pain, weakness, disappointment, suffering, unanswered prayers, death, to the Cross…

Reflect on Jesus' promise on the Cross: "Today you will be with me in Paradise" (Luke 23:43)…Image Jesus embracing each of your loved ones who has died and saying, "Today you will be with me in Paradise…"

Look into the resurrected face of Christ…Become filled with the dazzling light of God's glory shining in your life…in your body…in your relationships…in your hopes…in your dreams…in your future…See your loved ones as God sees them: radiant reflections of the divine image…Offer thanks for this vision of hope…

Pray for all people who suffer in any way in your family, neighborhood, community, church, city, nation, world... Ask Jesus to embrace each of these people with the courage and wisdom they need at this time...Consider how God may be calling you to do something to alleviate their suffering...Choose one person or group to serve...

PRAYER OF RELEASE

Relax for a few minutes in silence and become centered...Be aware of anything that keeps you from living in harmony with God and with other people...Let go of all distractions...Open yourself to God's presence dwelling within you...

Select one of the following relationships for reflection: relationships in which you have experienced unrequited love, a broken relationship, an abusive or addictive relationship...Observe how reflecting on this relationship influences your thoughts and feelings...

Ask God to do for you what you cannot do for yourself by releasing this person and yourself from any bondage, dependency, or abusive behavior pattern that exist within the relationship...Surrender these blockages to God... Cast away the darkness of your life...Remove sinful desires...Believe in Divine Power within you to lift the burdens of your heart...to increase your understanding... to enlighten your mind...

Release this person by name to God's loving care: "Loving God, I release (N.) to you. I let her(him) go free of any ties that bind. I accept her(his) choices and decisions. I affirm my decision for health and wholeness in this relationship. I ask you to remove this burden from my heart. I ask forgiveness for my failures in loving (N.). I offer forgiveness to (N.) for failing in loving me. I pray that you embrace (N.) and me this day with mercy and compassion. I set (N.) free and pray that peace, healing, and love will fill her(him)..."

See a figure coming toward you...Hear the figure call your name and say, "You are free. (Name of person you want to release) is free. I take away the darkness of the past that you shared. Both of you are forgiven. I cleanse your hearts and minds. I embrace both of you with healing, strength, wisdom, and courage. I fill both of you with peace. I send my angels to bless and protect both of you always. I want to live most fully and love most deeply within both of you." Recognize the voice of God speaking directly to you...

As you bring this prayer experience to a close, be aware of any feelings, images, insights, or sensations that emerge. Write, draw, or express your feelings, images, insights, or sensations in some creative way such as art, music, poetry, song, dance—anything God has revealed to you that helps you release other people, respect their choices, accept them as they are, forgive them, pray for their healing, and let go of the relationship. You might want to compose a psalm or litany of thanksgiving expressing your gratitude for God's liberating power in your life.

Finally, offer a prayer of blessing for the person you named in this reflection. For example, "God, embrace (N.) with deep peace, lasting joy, and eternal love. Amen." If appropriate, you may wish to share your prayer of blessing with this person.

 **FURTHER REFLECTION**

INDIVIDUAL

How do I feel when I let go and let God in times of suffering and pain?

How can Prayer of the Sufferer help me release myself from the pain of a relationship?

How can I grow spiritually by letting go of relationships that are addictive, compulsive, or broken?

How do I deal with unanswered prayers?

GROUP

How can Prayer of the Sufferer help us to let go and let God?

How can Prayer of the Sufferer help us release painful relationships to God's liberating power?

How can Prayer of the Sufferer help us find meaning in times of suffering?

In what areas of life can the Letting-Go-and-Letting-God Prayer and the Prayer of Release help us experience freedom and healing?

How can these prayers free us from unhealthy relationships with institutions and structures? For example, how can we experience freedom and healing from addictive, compulsive, relationships with Church? state? nation?

ABOUT *the* AUTHOR

Bridget Mary Meehan is a conference speaker, retreat and spiritual director. She is the author of twelve books including *Praying With Passionate Women*; *God Delights in You*; *Prayers, Activities, Celebrations for Catholic Families*; and *Contemplating Courageous Women*.